MW00817733

The Case for
the Christian Family

The Case for the Christian Family

The Covenantal Solution for the Dissolving American Family

JARED LONGSHORE

canonpress
MOSCOW, IDAHO

Published by Canon Press
P.O. Box 8729, Moscow, Idaho 83843
800.488.2034 | www.canonpress.com

Jared Longshore, *The Case for the Christian Family: The Covenantal Solution for the Dissolving American Family*
Copyright ©2022 by Jared Longshore

Cover design by James Engerbretson
Interior design by Valerie Anne Bost

Printed in the United States of America.

Unless otherwise noted, all Bible quotations are from the King James Version. All Bible quotations marked ESV are from the English Standard Version copyright ©2001 by Crossway Bibles, a division of Good News Publishers. Used by permission.

All rights reserved. No part of this publication may be reproduced, stored in a retrieval system, or transmitted in any form by any means, electronic, mechanical, photocopy, recording, or otherwise, without prior permission of the author, except as provided by USA copyright law.

Library of Congress Cataloging-in-Publication Data forthcoming

22 23 24 25 26 27 28 29 30 31   9 8 7 6 5 4 3 2 1

For Eric, Brenda, Arthur, and Rhoda.
We thank God for you, your faith,
and your covenant faithfulness.

Contents

Foreword

The center of our current cultural woes is found in a point of grammar. The vast majority of evangelicals have drifted into the erroneous idea that "the family" is an abstract noun. But for those steeped in the older biblical way of thinking, the family is a concrete noun—each one of them. It is a "thing" that exists objectively in the world, and is something that can be photographed. The chances are good that you have many such photographs around your house. The family is not a rarified floating concept that never really touches down.

Even though a lot of people think of the family this detached sort of way, it remains the case that we all have to go to bed somewhere, and so for many, home is simply where you hang your hat. But this is an arbitrary sort of thing, or so we think, and that is why we were extraordinarily docile when the Supreme Court decided in *Obergefell* to formulate (and foist) a radically new definition of marriage and family. But for many, since the family was thought to be just a matter of definition anyway, what could it matter if the editors of our cultural dictionary made some definitional adjustments?

Others did not like what was happening at all, but had no real categories for responding to it. They wanted to go to war, but discovered that they had no guns and no ammo.

What we are missing is the idea of *covenant*. This is what makes a family a *family*, and because God is the Lord of all covenants, God alone determines what a family is. God is the one who brought Eve to Adam in the first instance. And it was the Lord Jesus who said that in that act, God was not only joining Adam and Eve together, but also every married couple since that time (Matt. 19:6). What God has joined together, no man may put asunder on his own authority. We may go further and say that what God refuses to join together, man has no authority to attempt on his own.

The book you are holding promises to unsettle a lot of modern assumptions about marriage and family. I hope you are ready for that, because we are in desperate need of having a lot of modern assumptions unsettled. May God be with you as you prepare to do a lot of hard thinking.

Douglas Wilson
Christ Church, 2022

Introduction

The argument of this book is quite simple. The brass tacks solution to the dissolving American family is a recovery of the covenant household. Without such a recovery, the storm of secularism will wash away what is left of our eroding homes. Many Christians in the United States feel a bit like Davy Crockett and the Texans surrounded by Santa Anna at the Alamo. I thank God for the courage of these faithful conservatives. They stand ready to fight and die, win or lose. But I commend a plan to win in these pages. You, of course, will still have to die. We are Christians. We take up the cross. But there is a world of difference between dying in defeat and dying in victory.

The spirit of the age animates its devotees more vehemently than in days gone by. We are in a season of reaping. You can see the fruitful labors of these invisible ugly *isms* on nearly every segment of the nightly news.

But these demons have been sowing their doctrines in our land for decades. Christians have imbibed too much of their teaching and it has undone our families. We reap what we have sown and the only creatures pleased with the harvest are dung beetles. The putrid aroma wafting over the fields serves as an unsavory testimony to the fact that we are not doing it right. We cannot be mad that Joe Biden's Department of Children and Families will soon knock on our door to inform us that our children do not belong to us anymore. We have been raising orphans for years, long before the state agreed with our general sentiment that our children are bastards.

This book is a call for the vast majority of American evangelicals to go in a new direction, albeit it is an old path. But that path is long overgrown with oaks, palmettos, and shrubs of various kinds. Many have forgotten this old covenantal road. Others have never heard of it even though our fathers walked it faithfully for centuries. We, however, are deep into the forest now. So my tool of choice for the journey before us is a machete, not a scalpel. When you are finished with this book, I make no promise that you will be out of the woods. If you insist on *seeing the end* of this path before walking it, then you may be unsatisfied with the work you hold in your hands. If, on the other hand, you are willing to walk by faith and not by sight like our father Abraham, then this book may give you just the clarity you need to head out with your family in a new and better direction—"By faith Abraham obeyed when he was called to go out to a place that he was to receive as an inheritance. And he went out, not knowing where he was going" (Heb. 11:8, ESV).

My aim is to chop away some of the initial brush and point to the well-worn covenantal path that leads out of this Mirkwood. Here is what you can expect in pursuit of that end.

Chapter 1 sounds the alarm that we have lost the covenant household. It also signals how we fumbled this gift from God. We simply no longer think of the family the way Scripture speaks of the family and this covenantal-amnesia stems from ingesting the hollow and deceptive philosophies of our age (Col. 2:8).

Chapter 2 addresses covenant marriage between man and woman. That modifier "covenant" does not describe a mere approach to marriage. It describes the marriage institution itself as a divine act resulting in changes to the very nature of physical and spiritual reality. You can find several marriage books that speak to roles and responsibilities. But I address something more central and fundamental in this chapter: Through covenant, God makes husband and wife one. Then he proceeds to deal with them covenantally as one.

Chapter 3 turns to God's marriage with his bride (the covenant of grace). This chapter defines God's marriage covenant with his people and unearths the essential, organic connection between God's marriage with his bride and a man's marriage with his own. Many writers have described the "likeness" of marriage between man and woman and God's marriage with his bride. John Piper, for example, speaks of marriage as a parable of something permanent.[1] I do not want to say less. But I will say more. Our Christian marriages are more than a shadow of a heavenly reality. They are more than parabolically related to the covenant of grace.

Chapter 4 builds upon chapters 2 and 3, demonstrating that covenant children are in the covenant household. God not only deals with husband and wife as one. He deals with the fruit of such a union as one. The point of this chapter is not merely that God makes special promises to the Christian's children. The point is that if a covenant household finds itself in the covenant of grace, then the covenant children in such a household find themselves also in the covenant of grace.

Having made it this far, we hopefully have atomized, expressive, individualistic evangelicals reunited in covenant families. Moreover, these covenantal families have a sense that they are a covenant household within God's covenant of grace with his people. As we clear more of this ancient path out of this dark wood, chapter 5 uncovers the truth about God's kingdom. More particularly, it addresses the relationship between this covenantal household and the kingdom of God on earth. By the end of chapter 5, the encouragement should be flowing that we are not isolated individuals and neither are we isolated families. We are rather a kingdom of families making our way out of this pagan wilderness.

1. John Piper, *This Momentary Marriage* (Wheaton, IL: Crossway), 2012.

Chapter 6 commends covenant education for covenant households. God's design of the covenant house necessitates this particular form of education. On the one hand, many Christian homes have abdicated their ministry of education and handed it over to the state. On the other hand, some Christians who speak the language of covenant have neglected covenant nurture, falling into covenantal presumption. This ministry of the covenant house, namely covenant education, is an essential component to the restoration of the dissolving American family.

Chapter 7 depicts the covenant and the battle for the cosmos. That war rages in the United States at the moment. Two competing visions pitch themselves in combat with no signs of either side letting up. The first is a Christian vision grounded in God's covenant. The latter is a pagan vision grounded in nothing but the will and purposes of the creature. This conflict is no surprise. From the beginning, our Lord announced that the seed of the woman would be at enmity with the seed of the serpent. The covenant of grace is briefly traced through redemptive history, starting with God's establishment of that covenant with Adam and his house immediately upon the fall of mankind. God has kept his covenant promise to Adam, Noah, Abraham, Moses, David, and ultimately Christ. He will likewise keep his promises to us and to our children and in so doing he remakes the world. Our future conquest involves keeping the covenant by faith just as our fathers did.

So what do I hope you will do after turning the final page of this short book? Well, you must recall our present location. We are lost deep in an overgrown forest. Some books are helpful on a "how-to" practical level. They aim for readers to walk in a certain manner. My goal is far more humble. This book is not focused on how to walk on this path. It is more concerned with you discovering it and taking a few steps down this covenantal road. I have not made a grand discovery. Not only did our fathers walk this way for generations, but it would be fair to say I stumbled upon this path. You might say I was walking on it before I knew what it was. Then the lamp for my feet illuminated the terrain. My hope and prayer is that you would experience this same illumination.

1 Covenant Lost

Your Children Don't
Belong to You Anymore

I n this first chapter, I'm attempting a bit of shock and
awe. I'm going to say something that should give you
a jolt. After the jolt, I want to explore a bit to discover
how we got into such troubled waters. The culprit will not
be something entirely outside of us that we can point our
finger at in an act of self-justification. The ultimate culprit
for example is not Hilary Clinton saying, "It takes a vil-
lage . . . your children belong to us, you deplorables." I do
not deny that she is a threat. I contend that she is more.
She is a troubling manifestation of our own ideology. By
"our" in the previous sentence, I mean run-of-the-mill conservative Christians who still make up a majority of these
United States. The truth is we gave birth to Hillary Clinton.
She is the fruit of that drunken night when we went to bed

with hollow philosophy, vain deceit, the tradition of men, and the rudiments of the world (Col. 2:8).

If we are upset with the outcome, and we ought to be upset with the outcome, then we need to get out of that idolatrous bed. I'll help get us moving quicker from that bed with the aforementioned jolt: Legally speaking, your children don't belong to you anymore. That's how a legal friend of mine put it to me. The family has been dissolved as far as modern legal interpretation is concerned. This dissolution of the family will be further explained shortly. Before getting there, I admit that the total erosion of the family will take time to manifest itself in judicial decisions and the Living God can always turn things around. But the leaven is in the lump. Here's how it went down.

Everyone decided to heed Lennon when he said to imagine there is no heaven above us and no hell below us. We imagined that which is contrary to reality. To run the basics again, there indeed is a heaven above us and a hell below us. Lennon told us to pretend, and we decided to imagine with him. We forgot the actual state of things and decided to live contrary to nature. We discovered that once you start to live contrary to nature, the result is Berkley Law professors on the floor of the United States Senate insisting that men can get pregnant.[1] You can play the imagine game with more than just heaven and hell.

---

1. Jo Yurcaba, "Law professor Khiara Bridges calls Sen. Josh Hawley's questions about pregnancy 'transphobic.'" NBC News, July 13, 2022, https://www.nbcnews.com/nbc-out/out-politics-and-policy/law-professor -khiara-bridges-calls-sen-josh-hawleys-questions-pregnanc-rcna38015.

Imagine yourself, man, to be a woman. It is easy if you try. So man has forgotten what he is, and in his pride, he has insisted that everyone else forget with him. But, humans are not satisfied with the way of negation. This spirit of the age is not content with you simply forgetting the truth. You must be educated in falsehood. You must say the pronouns. You must speak the error. You must not worship your God and you must worship the false god being presented to you. This debased mind has wormed its way into our legal analysis, particularly and most recently via *Obergefell v. Hodges*.

Obergefell held that the right for same-sex couples to marry is a fundamental right inherent in the liberty of the person. That reasoning is, of course, nonsensical. It is a fundamental right inherent in the liberty of circles to have no sides. Triangles, according to nature, are free to have points. These liberties are inherent in the shapes themselves. You have such liberties, but the liberty for you to be a giraffe at the zoo is not numbered among them. Moreover, by granting the citizenry a faux and fabricated "right," the state attempts to strip her citizens of a fundamental one, namely family rights—and this will be explained further momentarily. *Obergefell*, then, is a gateway drug that results in the state exercising more and illegitimate authority over the people who are strung-out like crackheads needing another faux-right fix. This pattern leads to the dissolving of what truly belongs to you.

Parenthood is inextricably connected to marriage, so if you toy with marriage, scratch that, if you put a stick of dynamite in marriage and blow it to smithereens, then you inevitably do the same to parenthood. Not long after *Obergefell* ruled that same-sex couples have the constitutional right to marriage, there was an attempt to say that same-sex couples had the right to be parents to children who popped up amid their "marriage." Now, a normal man would ask, "How in the world does a child pop up in a same-sex 'marriage'?" Well, in the case of a lesbian relationship, one of the ladies can be artificially inseminated with a random man's semen. Yes, writing things like that gives you the Orwellian shakes. But, this is what happened in the real world. The Supreme Court case was called *Pavan v. Smith.*

Coming up to the Supreme Court from the state of Arkansas, *Pavan v. Smith* involved a lesbian couple, one of whom was artificially inseminated with a random man's semen. According to Arkansas, the inseminated woman would be listed as a parent on the birth certificate, but not that woman's lesbian partner. The ladies wanted both of their names listed as parents on the birth certificate. The Supreme Court of the United States found that Arkansas law had made "birth certificates more than a mere marker of biological relationship," and they ruled in favor of the lesbian couple. In a *per curiam* decision, the Supreme Court said the following:

> "For the purposes of birth registration," that [Arkansas] statute says, "the mother is deemed to be the woman who gives birth to the child." . . . And "[i]f the mother was married at the time of either conception or birth,"

the statute instructs that "the name of [her] husband shall be entered on the certificate as the father of the child."... There are some limited exceptions to the latter rule—for example, another man may appear on the birth certificate if the "mother" and "husband" and "putative father" all file affidavits vouching for the putative father's paternity... But as all parties agree, the requirement that a married woman's husband appear on her child's birth certificate applies in cases where the couple conceived by means of artificial insemination with the help of an anonymous sperm donor.[2]

In other words, the Supreme Court found the Arkansas Code to require the husband of a pregnant woman to be named on the child's birth certificate, even if he was not the biological father. Then the Supreme Court sunk in the hook,

Arkansas has thus chosen to make its birth certificates more than a mere marker of biological relationships: The State uses those certificates to give married parents a form of legal recognition that is not available to unmarried parents. Having made that choice, Arkansas may not, consistent with *Obergefell*, deny married same-sex couples that recognition.[3]

2. *Pavan v. Smith*, 582 U.S. 2 (2017), https://www.supremecourt.gov/opinions/16pdf/16-992_868c.pdf.
3. Ibid., 4.

Interestingly, the Arkansas Code stands amid a long legal tradition of assuming that the husband of the pregnant woman is the father. This presumed paternity only stands to reason within the structure of heterosexual marriage. This tradition accords with the sacredness of the marriage institution. But when that sacred institution is mocked and a foolish imposter poses as the genuine article, any attempt to carry over presumed paternity is tomfoolery on its face. The imposter of same-sex marriage lacks the essential components to beget children and thus any natural paternity or maternity for that matter is by nature itself excluded.

The *Pavan* case signals a rising change in legal reasoning. Parenthood is less and less being conceived of as a natural status, a sacred right and duty. It is being reduced to a status which comes into existence by mere intention. Intent-based parenting means that you can be a father *if you intend to be,* and this means that humans will be tasked with the job of determining such intent. So you may very well intend to be father to your child, but maybe someone else does, too. That someone else could have more victim identities than you do. Some of you, in fact, are straight, white, and male, which means you need to sit down and be quiet while we elevate other voices.

Now you might object here and say, "Parental rights don't seem to be based on intent because in the case above the parental rights were based on 'same-sex marriage.'" But here's the problem with that objection. "Same-sex marriage" is not real. No such thing exists. It is a vapor.

No, vapor is real. "Same-sex marriage" is less than a vapor; it is a no-thing. The objection above amounts to saying, "Parental rights are based on unicorns." The true basis in *Pavan v. Smith* is the "want to" of the lesbian couple (not to mention the fear and folly of the justices). Statism permeates this intent-based parenting for it redefines a pre-political institution into a post-political one. Now conservatives are whole-heartedly against such a set up. But most do not see how we have left the door open for such a development. Say the state comes knocking on your door. They are there for your children, and they explain to you that your children do not belong to you anymore. How do you respond? "Well," you say, "I would respond by pointing to my twelve-gauge and kindly reminding the state that the children do indeed belong to me." If this is your response, then God bless you and may your tribe increase. But aside from the shotgun, *on what grounds do your children belong to you?* I see two insufficient ways that conservatives would answer this question.

The first insufficient way, and my guess is this would be the less common response, is to claim that the children belong to you because you claim they do—"I feed them. I've agreed to be their father. They're under my roof, aren't they?" This claim puts the grounding at the level of individual consent (the parent) rather than state consent. The problem is that such reasoning is still based on intent, albeit individual intent. This individual intent approach will inevitably grow into statism for it founds the very category of fatherhood and motherhood merely on the human will.

The second insufficient way that conservatives would respond to the DCF agent at their door is as follows. The father would say, "These are my kids because they have my eyes, can't you see?" His argument would run along biological lines, "I don't need a theology degree. And I don't need a political science degree. I slept with their mother however many years ago and nine months later this little one came out." This rationale grounds parental authority in the paternity test and it is rooted in the notion of blood. Americans far and wide maintain the notion that blood is thicker than water. They understand kinfolk. But this approach, while grasping an essential and significant point, is insufficient. Many people may be surprised that I claim this second attempt to ward off the state's encroachment is insufficient. What is the problem with *merely* claiming the biological or blood relation?

Let me say first that the biological or blood relation is remarkably important. God has designed the world to run this way. The covenantal solution that I commend in this book is not at odds with the biological or natural family. They are in need of no reconciliation for they are good friends, close friends. I in no way want to introduce discord into a harmonious relationship. Moreover, we are in a time where our nation is being given over to a debased mind to do what is contrary to nature. Christians, then, need to give three cheers for nature, and that includes the natural family. The Apostle Paul understood how important kinfolk is, "For I could wish that myself were accursed from Christ for my brethren, my kinsmen according to the flesh" (Rom. 9:3). But the Apostle Paul also knew there was something that was more significant even than kinsmen according to the flesh. John the Baptist knew that God had a way of creating children supernaturally, "And think not to say within yourselves, We have Abraham to our father: for I say unto you, that God is able of these stones to raise up children unto Abraham" (Matt. 3:9). In other words, covenant family and the natural family are intended to be one in the same. Even so, the covenant family entails more than simply the biological.

Let me take another stab at detailing our present predicament, coming at it from another angle. This illustration may seem a little far afield, but stick with me. It will circle back around and hopefully land home. I'm going to tell you about four men in a bar: Christian Man, Rational Man, Postmodern Man, and Pagan Man. The man who grounds his parental authority merely in blood is the same man as Rational Man in the coming illustration. And take careful note of that word *merely* in the previous sentence. Mere Blood Man and Rational Man (who in essence are the same man) do not have the necessary resources to fight the good fight that is manifestly upon us. Far too many Christians have drifted to think and live as mere Rational and/or Blood Man and hence, we are in the trouble that we are in. Now for the illustration.

A Christian and a Rationalist walk into a bar. As they sit, they observe that there is in fact a blue chair beside them. Both men are agreed on the point, but for very different reasons. The Christian man explains that the chair is blue because God has made it so. God sustains it. And God's gracious hand so works that the two men can ascertain through human reason that it is so. Rational Man chuckles at the religious fervor of his friend and says, "Bud, the chair is blue, and it is self-evident that the chair is blue. I do not need all of this mumbo jumbo about God, creation, providence, and the present operation of his kindness in order to ascertain the simple fact that this most certainly is a chair and it is blue." This is the situation in which Americans have found themselves for some time. It was Christians and those who had some common sense. And everything was quite peaceful in this bar.

But eventually Postmodern Man walks into the bar and joins the conversation. He tells the two friends that they need to lighten up. The object in question may be a blue chair to them. But it might be a yellow sofa to someone else, and to another it might even be a green futon. Who is to say? To each their own, as the saying goes. Now Christian Man and Rational Man both know that Postmodern Man is out to lunch. But they have decided to put up with him. It seemed fine enough to put up with him because he was not holding a gun to anybody's head. He was just being a very strange man. At the end of the day, while the intellectual unity is falling apart in this friendly establishment, no one is throwing chairs or breaking beer bottles yet. We have been meandering along in this situation for a good while now also. But a new development is upon us.

A fourth man has walked into the bar and he goes by the name Pagan Man. As he enters, that old western duel music begins to play, the bartender ducks down behind the bar and the ladies scatter. He looks at the three men in the bar and says, "You are all wrong. That object there is a pink elephant. And you will all acknowledge it to be a pink elephant or off to the Gulag with you." Postmodern Man, who has been smoking the wonky weed this whole time, stands up to say, "Hey bro, lighten up because . . ." but he is swiftly backhanded in the mouth by Pagan Man, after which he falls to the ground mumbling something about it being OK because to somebody somewhere that slap was an act of love. Rational Man, observing the present threat, begins to inch closer and closer to Christian Man. He's starting to think he needs to hang his observations on something more than human reason. Christian Man is the only stable citizen in the bar who will stand up to the Pagan who insists that we all now call down up, the sun the moon, and Bruce Jenner a mother.

The fact is, a disenchanted, reductionistic Christianity, one shot through with pragmatism and tempted to live by reason alone, cannot survive in peacetime. It especially cannot survive when false gods show up. Picture your modern church growth guru standing with Ezekiel in that valley of dry bones. How long do you think he hangs around? Such a man is happy to package a movement that is already manifest. He can tailor and sell. But he doesn't have the simple faith for creation *ex nihilo* and hearts forming in the skeleton's chest. If he maintains his belief in angels and demons at all, he has relegated them to a heavenly sphere that has no impact on life in this world. The Christian Church in America needs to get its head around Lewis's point in *The Last Battle*. In that wonderful book, the idol Tash, a golden laden stone, showed up one day, walking, moving, living. An ape had called for Tash and Tash came—

> "It seems, then," said the Unicorn, "that there is a real Tash, after all." "Yes," said the Dwarf. "And this fool of an Ape, who didn't believe in Tash, will get more than he bargained for! He called for Tash: Tash has come . . . Ho, ho, ho!" chuckled the Dwarf, rubbing his hairy hands together. "It will be a surprise for the Ape. People shouldn't call for demons unless they really mean what they say."[4]

Sometimes when you call upon Tash, you get Tash. We miss this point because we are far too much like Rational Man. We have unhitched life on earth from the heavenlies. That is why we don't know what a father is.

But we have not *truly* unhitched life on earth from the heavens. Man cannot decouple life on earth from the heavenlies. You might as well attempt to disengage the Old and New Testaments, the soul and the body, the Spirit and the Word. But, we have pretended to do this very thing. What shocks us is that Pagan Man has not unhitched life on earth from the heavenlies. He is hooked up to the wrong side of the heavenlies, but hooked up he is.

4. C.S. Lewis, *The Last Battle* (New York: Harper Collins, 1956), kindle loc. 55.

Let me bring this point down upon parenting with a Bible verse that will hopefully make things plain. Your children are yours because the God of heaven gave them to you—"Lo, children are an heritage of the LORD: And the fruit of the womb is his reward" (Ps. 127:3). Commenting on this text, Calvin makes the point that something more than nature is going on here:

> Nothing seems more natural than for men to be produced of men. The majority of mankind dream, that after God had once ordained this at the beginning, children were thenceforth begotten solely by a secret instinct of nature, God ceasing to interfere in the matter; and even those who are endued with some sense of piety, although they may not deny that He is the Father and Creator of the human race, yet do not acknowledge that his providential care descends to this particular case, but rather think that men are created by a certain universal motion. With the view of correcting this preposterous error, Solomon calls children *the heritage of God*, and the fruit of the womb *his gift*; for the Hebrew word רכש, *sachar*, translated *reward*, signifies whatever benefits God bestows upon men, as is plainly manifest from many passages of Scripture. The meaning then is, that children are not the fruit of chance, but that God, as it seems good to him, distributes to every man his share of them.[5]

---

5. John Calvin and James Anderson, *Commentary on the Book of Psalms*, vol. 5 (Bellingham, WA: Logos Bible Software, 2010), 110.

What does all of this mean? It means your children are yours, not by might, nor by power, but by the Spirit of the LORD. The household is supernatural. It is the product of a divine action. To object to it, or to attempt to dissolve it, is not only contrary to nature. It is demonic rebellion against the Living God who rules the kingdom of men. It is an attempt to disband the covenant. One reason the present attempt to undo the family is seeing such success, is because Christians have for some time now disbanded the covenant themselves. Legally speaking, our children don't belong to us anymore. And that is because we ourselves have lived as if they do not.

The following pages are intended to change that.

2 Covenant Marriage
What God Has Joined Together

So chapter 1 was a sober warning: Legally speaking your children don't belong to you anymore. This tragic legal situation stems from the ungodly Supreme Court decision *Obergefell v. Hodges*. This degeneration is no surprise to us. If you don't get marriage right, then you can't get parenting right. But *Obergefell* itself stemmed from a worldview that disregarded heaven and the God who bows those heavens and comes down riding the cherub (Ps. 18:9-10).

Now you can still find people who will say that marriage is sacred. So if we would rouse man from his secular slumbers, then marriage is at least an opportunity for us to get our foot in the door. In spite of the assault we have leveled against this holy institution, you still have men and women walking away from a wedding ceremony knowing they tasted something potent. They may not be able to put their finger on it, but they were moved. By what? Well, the wind coming off the cherub's wing of course. God descended in their midst and made a covenant—"He did fly upon the wings of the wind" (Ps. 18:10).

This chapter starts the recovery of what we have lost by identifying the nature and significance of covenant marriage. As noted in the introduction, the focus of this chapter is not marital roles and responsibilities. Rather I will describe marriage itself from various angles and texts of Scripture. Then I will begin to identify some of the implications of man and woman being joined together in marriage. Those implications reach farther than many know. Any recovery of the dissolving American family must start right here with covenant marriage.

We might begin by coming at it from this angle. Marriage is more than the product of the will (the intent) of the parties involved. We are so steeped in our secular humanism that we really have taken on a sense of deity. We think that we are the sole creators of things. We have forgotten the fundamental truth that "in him we live and move and have our being" (Acts 17:28). Applied to marriage, we think marriage is something we create and God subsequently blesses. For instance, you could find many Christians saying that same-sex marriage is a real marriage that God won't bless. But such an expression signals a critical misunderstanding of the very nature of marriage. Same-sex marriage is not a marriage that God will not bless. Regardless of the intent of the parties, same-sex marriage is simply no marriage at all.

The essential text is, "What therefore God hath joined together, let not man put asunder" (Matt. 19:6). Think about that verse. It teaches that God really does join together: His hand does the joining. And the question naturally follows, "Does God join just anybody together in marriage?" The answer to that question is, no. God sets the terms and parameters of marriage. When God joins a man and woman in marriage, he creates a new thing that did not exist before. Prior to the marriage, you had Jack Thompson and Jill Williams. After the marriage you still have Jack and Jill. The new thing that you have—and note that "thing" is in the singular—is *the Thompsons*. The Thompsons are now a real thing. They are one new and real thing. The Thompsons did not exist before the marriage and the Thompsons do exist after the marriage.

God's creation of the Thompsons is something categorically different than the creation of a business arrangement. The former is a covenant and the latter is a contract. In other words, the former is something that God himself binds. To borrow an illustration from my friend Doug Wilson, say Jeff and Bob agree to a business deal in which Jeff will supply a hundred tractors and Bob will buy said tractors for X amount of dollars. They sign the contract, shake hands, and part ways. But three weeks later, Jeff's tractor manufacturing plant burns down and Bob is gifted a hundred tractors by a rich uncle who got out of the farming business up north. Neither man has a need for the contract anymore. They can come together, call it off without harm, foul, or sin.

But such is not the case with Jack and Jill above. Say three weeks after their marriage, it is not working out for either of them.

Well, tough.

They're not in a contract. They are in a covenant. God has joined them together. He has not merely overseen verbal commitments. He has actually created and bonded Jack and Jill such that they are now *the Thompsons*, and what God has joined together, let man not separate.

God proceeds to deal with the Thompsons as the Thompsons. The Thompsons are a unit, and he deals with them as a unit. My point is not that Jack and Jill give up their Jackness or their Jillness. They are indeed still individuals before the Living God. But they are not merely individuals before the living God. They are also the Thompsons before the Living God and Jack is the head of the Thompsons.

Ephesians 5:23 says, "For the husband is the head of the wife, even as Christ is the head of the church: and he is the saviour of the body." So Jack is the head and representative of his wife. For this reason, God went to Adam first after he and his wife Eve ate the fruit. The point is not that wives are exempt from all responsibility. The point is that Adam bore the primary responsibility because he was established by God as the head of his wife. God went and confronted Eve after he confronted Adam. But the covenantal headship is established in the order of God's dealings with our first parents.

When children come along, they are not born into this world as mere individuals. They are born into this world with a last name. They are born into this world a Thompson. It was not too long ago that our culture remembered this. You likely have a father or a grandfather who would remind you when he was dropping you off for Little League practice that you were indeed a Thompson. That last name came with certain privileges and responsibilities.

Jonathan Burnside has explained that for biblical Israel

> family was conventionally understood as a series of increasingly large kinship circles, beginning with the smallest social unit, the "father's house" and moving outwards in ever-increasing circles to include clan and tribe. Textual support for this is found in Joshua 7:14-18 where Joshua calls the nations of Israel forward by tribe, clan, and household in order to identify a particular individual. The family in ancient Israel is thus an example of a "patrilineal, segmentary, lineage system." The "father's house" is frequently referred to in biblical law (e.g., Deuteronomy 22:21).[1]

It follows that an attempt to tear down the patriarchy is an attempt to undo the divine design of marriage. It is an attempt to undo a divinely established covenant, and this assault on God's design has been going on for some time. All the way back in 1971, the Gay Liberation Manifesto admitted, "Equality is never going to be enough. What

---

1. Jonathan Burnside, *God, Justice, and Society: Aspects of Law and Legality in the Bible* (New York: Oxford University Press, 2010), 317.

is needed is a total social revolution, a complete reordering of civilization. Including society's most basic institution, the patriarchal society."[2] Around that same time, Kate Millet, a leader in the second wave of feminism in America, gathered for assemblies in which the following call and response was heralded:

"Why are we here today?"

"To make revolution," they answered.

"What kind of revolution?" she replied.

"The Cultural Revolution," they chanted.

"And how do we make Cultural Revolution?" she demanded.

"By destroying the American family!" they answered.

"How do we destroy the family?" she came back.

"By destroying the American Patriarch," they cried exuberantly.

"And how do we destroy the American Patriarch?" she replied.

"By taking away his power!"

"How do we do that?"

"By destroying monogamy!" they shouted.

"How can we destroy monogamy?"

"By promoting promiscuity, eroticism, prostitution, and homosexuality!" they resounded.[3]

2. Manifesto Group, *Gay Liberation Front Manifesto* (London: Gay Liberation Front, 1971).
3. Mallory Millett, "Marxist Feminism's Ruined Lives," *Frontpage Magazine*, September 1, 2014, https://www.frontpagemag.com/marxist-feminisms-ruined-lives-mallory-millett/.

The point that you must see is not merely that this is high-handed rebellion against God. It is that. But you must see that this is an attempt to break apart God's bonds. It is an attempt to undo a divinely bonded entity called the covenant house. We already know God's response, "He who sits in the heavens laughs" (Ps. 2:4). Legally, this means that if a man shows up before the magistrate of a given town and says, "I want to put my wife away," then that magistrate should ask, "Do you have cause?" When the man says that he does not have cause, then the magistrate must not grant the divorce. Now, that world is not the one we are living in. No-fault divorce means that the magistrate will grant the divorce without cause, and this cultural and civil situation stems directly from our rebellion against God.

Let's journey back to that bar with the four men: Christian Man, Rational Man, Postmodern Man, and Pagan Man, and let's exchange the object in question from a blue chair to a marriage. For a long time, Christian Man and Rational Man said that the marriage between one man and one woman was a marriage. The Christian maintained this covenantal idea that I'm addressing in this chapter: that man and that woman are bound in marriage because God has made it so and continues to sustain it. Rational man doesn't buy the God mumbo jumbo, but he has respect for marriage between one man and one woman. He says, "It is self-evident that this is a marriage. I watched the vows: there indeed is one man and one woman, that's all you need, partner." Postmodern Man walked in insisting that the real location of marriage was in the heart. You don't need the vows, families, or witnesses. You just need to feel like you're married and you're good to go. But now Pagan Man has walked in pointing to a man and a man and saying, "This is a marriage, and you will bake the wedding cake, or you will be frog-marched to the Gulag."

That illustration shows how we have gotten into the mess we are in: If you sever the covenantal idea, then everything goes haywire. If you think that marriage merely consists in human vows (Rational Man), then you will end up at gay marriage, or marriage to a robot for that matter. And yes, that has really happened.[4] We really do need to turn things around. And the only way to do that is to recover a true vision of marriage, covenant marriage.

COVENANT MARRIAGE

I am not coining the term *covenant marriage*. I'm not putting the adjective on marriage and then commending you think of it as one approach of many. Dieting is a thing, and a keto diet is one approach. I'm not recommending covenant marriage as a particular approach. I'm simply telling you what marriage *is*. Marriage is covenant marriage. How do we know that to be true?

4. Benjamin Haas, "Chinese Man 'Marries' Robot He Built Himself," *The Guardian*, April 4, 2017, https://www.theguardian.com/world/2017/apr/04/chinese-man-marries-robot-built-himself.

We know this is true because God himself calls marriage a covenant. He rebukes his people saying, "The LORD hath been witness between thee and the wife of thy youth, against whom thou hast dealt treacherously: yet is she thy companion, and *the wife of thy covenant*" (Mal. 2:14, emphasis added). The Hebrew word used there for covenant carries the sense of an alliance or a league. This alliance is a real alliance, a real league, a real thing. Malachi tells us some important things about this marriage covenant.

First, God is the originator of this covenant. If you ask, "Where does this covenant come from? Who established it, ordered it, arranged it?" the answer is, God did. That's what Malachi means when he says, "And did not he make one?" (Mal. 2:15). Malachi refers to God making one woman, Eve, not two, or three, or four. The men of Judah had entered into polygamy, marrying foreign women—"for Judah hath profaned the holiness of the LORD which he loved, and hath married the daughter of a strange god" (Mal. 2:11). Malachi, then, points back to the original marriage designed by God.

The language of the prophet is tricky. So know that I'm not venturing a novel interpretation here. John Calvin says of this verse,

> So now our Prophet reasons, *Has not God made one?* that is, "consider within yourselves whether God, when he created man and instituted marriage, gave many wives to one man? By no means. Ye see then that spurious and contrary

to the character of a true and pure marriage is everything that does not harmonize with its first institution."[5]

By pointing Judah back to God's original design, he is not merely saying, "You should do it the way God did it," as if God's original is the substance back there and our marriages today are a shadow that ought to look like the original prototype. Rather, Malachi points to *the very nature* of the abiding marriage institution. In Calvin's words, "the institution of marriage is a perpetual law."[6]

With this foundation laid, we can gain a right understanding of what Malachi means by saying that God is "witness between thee and the wife of thy youth" (Mal. 2:14). The point is not simply that God witnesses your marriage like the family, church, and friends that gather to witness your marriage. God is witness *between* husband and wife. He is a party to the marriage covenant. He is the one who solemnly joins husband and wife. He set the framework of the marriage covenant in the very beginning, and he conjoins every man and woman in marriage that has ever been conjoined.

What's more, God unites husband and wife in covenant marriage for a purpose. He has been doing so from the beginning. After announcing that God made them one, he asks, "And wherefore one? That he might seek a godly seed" (Mal. 2:15). The first thing to note is that

5. John Calvin and John Owen, *Commentaries on the Twelve Minor Prophets*, vol. 5 (Bellingham, WA: Logos Bible Software, 2010), 557.
6. Ibid., 556.

marriage exists for procreation. In the beginning, God said, "Be fruitful and multiply, and replenish the earth and subdue it" (Gen. 1:28). So begetting children is not a choice, but a command. But, even a surface-level reading of Malachi 2:15 signals that there is more involved than simple procreation.

Malachi says that God made one "that he might seek a godly seed." He is saying this to the covenant people of God who not only engaged in polygamy by seeking multiple wives, but married women "of a strange god" (Mal. 2:11). That is, men in God's covenant married women outside of God's covenant. When they did so, God said of such men, "The LORD will cut off the man that doeth this, the master and the scholar, out of the tabernacles of Jacob" (Mal. 2:12). The resulting situation was not good at all. The men, who were in covenant with God, were cut off from covenant with God. The women themselves who became pregnant from such a union were not in covenant with God for they were worshippers of a strange god. It follows that the children born of such a union would not be "godly seed." And this whole direction, according to Malachi, is contrary to God's original design of covenant marriage.

God's design of marriage for the purpose of "holy seed" is not only found in the Old Testament. The same principle appears in the Apostle Paul's admonitions to the Corinthians. In 1 Corinthians 7:12-14, Paul writes,

> If any brother hath a wife that believeth not, and she be pleased to dwell with him, let him not put her away. And

the woman which hath an husband that believeth not, and if he be pleased to dwell with her, let her not leave him. For the unbelieving husband is sanctified by the wife, and the unbelieving wife is sanctified by the husband: else were your children unclean; but now are they holy.

The same "holy seed" principle is at play in Malachi and 1 Corinthians. But the circumstances are different. In Malachi 2, the warning is against contracting marriage with an unbeliever. 1 Corinthians 7 does not speak to contracting marriages, but dealing with marriages that are already contracted in which there is a Christian and an unbeliever. Calvin, for example, writes,

Let us, however, bear in mind, that he speaks here not of contracting marriages, but of maintaining those that have been already contracted; for where the matter under consideration is, whether one should marry an unbelieving wife, or whether one should marry an unbelieving husband, then that exhortation is in point—*Be not yoked with unbelievers, for there is no agreement between Christ and Belial.* (2 Cor. 6:14.) But he that is already bound has no longer liberty of choice; hence the advice given is different.[7]

The question was, "Should the Christian man remain married to the unbeliever now that he has become a Christian?" Paul admonishes the Christian husband not

7. John Calvin and John Pringle, *Commentaries on the Epistles of Paul the Apostle to the Corinthians,* vol. 1 (Bellingham, WA: Logos Bible Software, 2010), 241.

to put away his unbelieving wife, and he admonishes the Christian wife not to leave her unbelieving husband. One reason for this is that their children would be unclean if they did so. As it is, even with one spouse an unbeliever, the children of such a marriage are holy given the Christianity of one parent. That passage of Scripture sounds very strange to evangelical ears. The first thing to be said is that this sanctification and holiness spoken of does not refer precisely to the personal regeneration of the child. But, the sanctification and holiness spoken of is real sanctification and holiness. A trustworthy Greek lexicon defines the word *sanctify* found in the passage above as, "to include a person in the inner circle of what is holy, in both cultic and moral associations of the word."[8]

In other words, the children of a believer are brought into the gracious covenant of God. This same "sanctification" terminology is employed in Hebrews 10:29 where God's covenant of grace is explicitly mentioned, "Of how much sorer punishment, suppose ye, shall he be thought worthy, who hath trodden under foot the Son of God, and hath counted the blood of the covenant, *wherewith he was sanctified*, an unholy thing, and hath done despite unto the Spirit of grace?" (emphasis mine).

You can also see that the one who is sanctified by the blood of the covenant, namely Jesus' blood, can be

8. William Arndt et al., *A Greek-English Lexicon of the New Testament and Other Early Christian Literature* (Chicago: University of Chicago Press, 2000), 10.

sanctified by the blood of that covenant and walk away from it, trampling over the Son of God himself, receiving a great punishment. In other words, this person in view in Hebrews 10:29 was not personally born again, but he or she was sanctified by the blood of the covenant. This sanctification by the blood of the covenant is the very thing in view when Paul speaks of the children of a believer. Such children are sanctified by the blood of the covenant. They are in the covenant of grace. These children are "holy seed."

Malachi 2 and 1 Corinthians 7 indicate the significance of covenant marriage, even when it comes to the status of one's children as holy or unclean. That status is not merely a matter of biology. Wedlock plays an essential role. As I mentioned in chapter 1, God has designed the biological or natural family and the covenantal family to be but different dimensions of the one same family. Our sin introduces the discord. The following example of that discord highlights the significance of covenant marriage.

Posit a single man, Bob Johnson, and a married couple, John and Jane Doe. One night Bob commits adultery, taking John's wife, Jane. If the woman discovered later that she was pregnant with a child, to whom would that child belong? Blood says that the single man who is undoubtedly related to the child biologically is in essence the only real father. But those who understand the covenant say something different.

Bob has no authority over Jane with whom he has committed adultery. They engaged in the act that is designed to be the consummation of the marriage covenant. But they in fact were not bound in a marriage covenant. The woman was bound in a marriage covenant to her husband. The husband, John Doe, is head of his wife who is now with child. This wife truly belongs to her head. She is his body (Eph. 5:23). She now has a living human in her womb. So Bob Johnson is not the head of Jane Doe because John Doe is the head of Jane, and it follows that Bob has no authority over the child in Jane's womb either. He indeed has certain duties to Jane and the child. He must provide resources to her for the provision of the child. But Jane and her child do not belong to Bob. John Doe is the head of Jane, and he is warranted the first right of headship to the child in his wife's womb.

This illustration demonstrates that blood is not the sole and ultimate thing or the end of the matter. If Bob said, "I am this child's father because he has my eyes, my features, and my blood," he would be right about the eyes, features, and blood, and he would be wrong about the conclusion that such makes him the legitimate father of the child. Bob cannot say, "As for my house," and have the child in question be included. The child is not a part of his covenantal house no matter the blood relation. I should note that I am not denying that there is a special relationship between Bob and the child. I am saying that the blood relation, in such a sinful and convoluted circumstance, does not make him a covenant father. The covenantal household is a truth that, while designed to flow with the biological like the stream does with the largemouth bass, can itself never be reduced to the fish.

Taking this same illustration, now posit that Bob is a Christian and John and Jane Doe are unbelievers. If John and Jane have a child, that child is not in covenant with God. John and Jane are not in God's covenant of grace, and it follows that their child is not either. If Bob (the Christian) married a Christian woman, the child of that union would be holy, in God's covenant of grace (1 Cor. 7:12-14). If Bob committed adultery by taking John's wife, Jane, Bob the Christian would not be the covenant head of that child, even though he is biologically the one who sired the child. John would have the first right of headship, and if he assumed that right, then neither father, mother, nor child would be holy, in God's covenant of grace. Similarly, if John divorced his wife on grounds of adultery, then Jane would become the head of the child, not John and not Bob. In this case, Jane being an unbeliever, the child would still not be holy, a member in God's covenant of grace.

This point is important to see because, as important as blood is, and as harmonious and interrelated it is to covenant, covenant and headship cannot be reduced to blood. The covenant house and headship are ultimately about the work of God when he joins man and woman together in marriage. All of this needs to be explained further. Malachi 2 and 1 Corinthians 7 signal that the marriage covenant between one man and one woman is very much related to God's gracious covenant with his bride. So to this latter covenant, the covenant of grace, we now turn.

3 Covenant Grace

To Be God to You and Your Children

The Bible says a good deal about covenant marriage, and if you survey Scripture on the topic of marriage, you will find that marriage between one man and one woman is not the only marriage we hear about. We also hear about God's covenant marriage with his bride:

Turn, O backsliding children, saith the Lord; for I am married unto you. (Jer. 3:14)

For thy Maker is thine husband; The Lord of hosts is his name; And thy Redeemer the Holy One of Israel; The God of the whole earth shall he be called. (Isa. 54:5)

And I John saw the holy city, new Jerusalem, coming down from God out of heaven, prepared as a bride adorned for her husband. (Rev. 21:2)

For this cause shall a man leave his father and mother, and shall be joined unto his wife, and they two shall be one flesh. This is a great mystery: but I speak concerning Christ and the church. (Eph. 5:31-32)

God's marriage to his people is likened to a man's marriage to his wife. These are two covenants. The former is God's covenant of grace with his covenant people. The latter is a marriage covenant between man and woman that God himself establishes. These two covenants, the covenant of grace and the marriage covenant, are not unrelated. We know this to be the case already from Malachi 2. The men of Judah profaned the covenant of their fathers (Mal. 2:10), and they did so by marrying the daughters of a strange god (Mal. 2:11). The result was that such men were "cut off" out of "the tabernacles of Jacob" (Mal. 2:12). So a man's outright unfaithfulness in his marriage covenant resulted in him being cut off from God's gracious covenant with his bride. Moreover, such sin transgressed God's original design for "holy seed."

Chapter 2 signaled the relationship between covenant marriage and the covenant of grace. However, we still need a full definition of the covenant of grace, as well as an analysis of the organic relationship it maintains with covenant marriage. The main thread of this book is that the solution to the dissolving American family is a recovery of the covenant house. But there will be no genuine recovery of the covenant house without a recovery of God's covenant with his house, the covenant of grace.

There will be no rebuilding of the American family if we do not build it organically upon God's covenant of grace. As I noted before, our Christian marriages are more than a shadow of a heavenly reality (God's covenant with his bride). They are more than parabolically related to the covenant of grace. They are not one and the same thing, of course. But they are related such that Joshua had a right to say, "As for me and my house, we will serve the Lord."

We must begin with a definition for the covenant of grace. Defining the covenant of grace is no easy task. It is something akin to defining the word *mother*. What is a mother? Well, where do you start? The concept is too glorious for a sentence. But I'll do my best by starting with an illustration and then putting some words together in a sentence in an attempt to capture the concept.

The covenant of grace is likened to an ice cream shop. Christ himself is the ice cream in this ice cream shop, "Taste and see that he is good" (Ps. 34:8). God serves ice cream in the ice cream shop. This is simply the way he has chosen to go about it. God's banner over this ice cream shop is directed to all those inside and it reads, "I am your God and you are my people." And the pronouns in "your" and "you" in the previous sentence are in the plural. When a man calls upon the name of the Lord, he enters the ice cream shop, and his household comes with him into the ice cream shop. And yes, it is true that not every person in this ice cream shop is actually eating the ice cream.

From the time of our fall in our father Adam, our God set up this gracious ice cream shop in which he served his people Christ, the ice cream. Ice cream eating, genuine and saving communion with Christ that is, has always been done by faith. At the coming of Christ in the flesh, he established a new form of this ice cream shop. Christ established a new ice cream shop structure over the old and the old has passed away. So there has only been one true ice cream shop throughout history, but there was a genuine change in the structure of this establishment and its administration (the New Covenant). Whether it be the old model or the new, this ice cream shop has served the same ice cream (Christ), housed the same people (covenant members), and it has always been a family-friendly establishment (i.e. when a man enters to eat the ice cream, his household comes into the shop with him).

Our muddledness on the marriage covenant is not un-related to our muddledness on God's covenant of grace. American Christians by and large envision not an ice cream shop, but an ice cream stand in the street. Jesus is being preached at this ice cream stand. Christ, the ice cream, is being served up, and individuals either eat or do not eat. But, no shop. On the one hand, this ice cream stand approach is not the end of the world. You still have the ice cream (Christ). And you have individuals eating or not eating. On the other hand, in this ice cream stand arrangement, any concept of covenant gets folded into eating the ice cream as an individual. To be in covenant with God is simply to eat the ice cream. Covenant is only an individual matter and covenant is reduced to God's effectual call of an individual in the order of salvation.

Covenant becomes simply God getting thing A to individual B (the ice cream to an individual eater). This notion falls short of a biblical definition of the covenant of grace. With this illustration before us, I will attempt a detailed definition: The covenant of grace is the Heavenly Father's solemn oath to man on earth of grace in and by Jesus Christ, conditioned upon obedient faith, that constitutes a legal and relational bond in blood, a community, and/or an organization over and to which God says, "I am your (plural) God and you (plural) are my people." That definition is full and it needs to be supported from Scripture, but there is a lot of text to cover. The word "covenant" appears 284 times in the Old Testament, and it appears 33 times in the New Testament. I won't cover every appearance of course, but we will examine a few below.

Consider a few things about that definition. First, I've made the point that it is the Heavenly Father who covenants with man on earth. That is because a divine covenant with man is executed in history. What is in view is not a platonic covenant. It is not *the idea* of a covenant. It is not a covenant up in the heavens. A covenant is cut. Covenants must be established or they are not divine covenants with man. You have no divine covenant with man if you don't have a bond in blood. Blood and people are essential ingredients in the covenant of grace. So the heavenly and earthly language, as well as the blood language, is a reminder that covenants originate with God in heaven and they are executed down here on earth with man.

Regarding blood, God's dealings with Abraham in Genesis 15 constitutes a clear example. The blood of the slain animals signals an intense and formal covenant established—

> A covenant is a bond-in-blood. It involves commitments with life-and-death consequences. At the point of covenantal inauguration, the parties of the covenant are committed to one another by a formalizing process of blood-shedding. This blood-shedding represents the intensity of the commitment of the covenant. By the covenant they are bound for life and death.[1]

Second, the covenant of grace involves the creation and formation of a constituted people. Theologians often use the language of administration, and that is fine language, but many can mistake such language to mean "getting thing A to individual B," as in "I administer lotion to my daughter's knee." That idea does not capture what is involved in the word administration. Rather, think of how we use the word administration when we refer to the Biden or Trump administration. The Biden or Trump *administration* refers to an entity, a people, an organization, a corporate reality. You can be a member of such an administration or not a member of such an administration. It sounds strange to speak of being a member of a covenant if a covenant is nothing more than God's promise to an individual. You might say

1. O. Palmer Robertson, *The Christ of the Covenants* (Phillipsburg, NJ: 1980), 14.

that you are a *believer* of the covenant. But covenant membership implies that a covenant is more than a promise, it is an administration, organization, or league. Membership in an administration involves rights and responsibilities. None of that comes through when we conceive of a covenant as a mere promise from God to an individual. Now, God makes promises to individuals. I'm not disputing that he does. I'm saying that to reduce covenant to such a notion is to do injustice to the covenant idea.

Third, and this point is closely related to the second, the covenant of grace involves a relationship between God and his covenant people over which he says, "I am your God and you are my people." As the definition indicates, those pronouns are plural. The second person plural doesn't come across well in English because it matches the second person singular in form (you and you). This causes us to read many passages thinking that the point is about us as individuals. We Americans make this mistake all the more often because of individualistic presuppositions. So by all means you are an individual, and you are an individual before the face of God. But that is not all that you are. As the good ole Southerners would say, you are also a y'all.

I've moved out of the South, but having lived my whole life there I've reflected with a chuckle about how the corporate operated in speech. Growing up, if you saw some friends out and about, you'd likely ask, "How y'all doing?" And when you asked the question, you were not only thinking about the people in front of you. Your friends were in view, yes, but if they were there, their folks were in view too: parents, grandparents, kids, and grandkids. That's a covenantal way of thinking. So the point to emphasize here is that the covenant of grace concerns man on earth, a real organization, and that organization or entity is not merely an individual, or even a collection of individuals, but a y'all—a one new man. We hear about this one new man in Ephesians 2:15, "Having abolished in his flesh the enmity, even the law of commandments contained in ordinances; for to make in himself of twain one new man." Interestingly, that text employs the same language we hear when God joins a man and woman together in covenant marriage. Ephesians 2:15 is not speaking to marriage between one man and one woman, but God's creating one new man with whom he enters into a covenant of grace.

Fourth, the covenant of grace maintains an eschatological orientation. It is not a static thing. It is the solemn oath of grace in and by Jesus Christ. But that does not mean that the covenant of grace *only* has in view your personal justification. Jesus came to save *the world*— "For God sent not his Son into the world to condemn the world; but that the world through him might be saved" (John 3:17). The covenant of grace regards the promise of the Father of grace, the increase of grace, grace upon grace, grace to the ends of the earth. Now, does this definition (and the ice cream shop illustration above) hold up?

Well, we might start by looking at a definition of the Hebrew word for covenant. One Hebrew-English lexicon defines *covenant* as an "alliance of friendship" and "a divine constitution or ordinance with signs and seals" between

God and man.[2] As noted before, this definition of covenant entails more than a promise. Alliance, league, and constitution are hovering right there at the heart of what a covenant is. We see something similar in the New Testament Greek word for covenant. A good Greek-English lexicon defines *covenant* as "last will and testament." And *covenant* "retains the component of legal disposition of personal goods while omitting that of the anticipated death of a testator."[3] So the point is not that the covenant involves God dying per se. But the covenant does involve God determining what to do with what is his, "You are my people, and here is what is going to happen with you."

As I mentioned before, the covenant of grace is found throughout the Scriptures. And the context in which it is used sheds light on the nature of God's covenant of grace. The friendship or relational sense comes through in Psalm 25:14, "The secret of the Lord is with them that fear him; And he will shew them his covenant." Here I would quibble with those who want to describe the covenant of grace in merely legal terms. The covenant of grace indeed has legal dimensions. But claiming that the covenant of grace is merely legal and not relational in any sense simply does not square with Scripture. David says that God will reveal his covenant to those who fear him like a friend shares a secret with his companion. When God covenants grace to

2. Francis Brown, Samuel Rolles Driver, and Charles Augustus Briggs, *Enhanced Brown-Driver-Briggs Hebrew and English Lexicon* (Oxford: Clarendon Press, 1977), 136.
3. William Arndt, *A Greek-English Lexicon*, 228.

Abraham, he promises "to be God unto thee, and thy seed after thee" (Gen. 17:7). That is relational language.

The corporate, constitutional, and eschatological dimensions of the covenant of grace are seen in a text like Genesis 9:8-9, "And God spake unto Noah, and to his sons with him, saying, 'And I, behold, I establish my covenant with you, and with your seed after you.'" God does not only make this covenant with Noah. He speaks unto Noah and to his sons with him. The covenant is corporate, involving more than the individual. Moreover, God's covenant maintains an eschatological scope, for God will establish his covenant with Noah's seed after him. The constitutional dimension of the covenant is seen in that God says he will establish his covenant with Noah. God is not simply making a promise to Noah. He is establishing a people to whom a promise is made.

We see these same things in God's covenant with Abraham. Genesis 15:18 says, "In the same day the LORD made a covenant with Abram, saying, Unto thy seed have I given this land, from the river of Egypt unto the great river, the river Euphrates." Again, God's covenant is not merely with Abram, but Abram's seed; thus it is corporate and familial in nature. Also, the covenant involves a bond: God "made a covenant with" Abram. He was not merely delivering a promise to Abram, he was establishing a bond with Abram and his seed. Similarly, the earthly component is seen in that God made covenant with Abram in a certain day, thus the covenant was historical in nature. And it, of course, was made with Abraham on earth.

COVENANT HOUSE IN THE COVENANT OF GRACE

We now have a definition of the covenant of grace. And we already have indicators lighting up the dashboard signaling that when a man enters the covenant of grace his household comes with him into that covenant with God. I have made that assertion above. That is not a novel claim. Herman Bavinck for example has said that the covenant of grace

> is never made with a solitary individual but always also with his or her descendants. It is a covenant from generations to generations. Nor does it ever encompass just the person of the believer in the abstract but that person concretely as he or she exists and lives in history, hence including everything that is his or hers. It includes him or her not just as a person but him or her also as father and mother, as parent or child, with all that is his or hers, with his or her family, money, possessions, influence, and power, with his or her office and job, intellect and heart, science and art, with his or her life in society and the state.[4]

This claim that the covenant of grace "is never made with a solitary individual but always also with his or her descendants" makes sense given the definition of the covenant of grace above. The claim does not make sense if one reduces the covenant of grace to effectual calling

---

4. Herman Bavinck, *Reformed Dogmatics,* vol. 3, *Sin and Salvation in Christ,* ed. John Bold and trans. John Vriend (Grand Rapids: Baker Academic, 2006), 230.

or personal regeneration. In that case, Bavinck's claim would be that your descendants are regenerated by God upon your regeneration. And the good Calvinists know that once regenerated, never unregenerated, lost, or condemned. It would follow, under the "covenant of grace equals regeneration" scheme that all natural descendants of the regenerate would be robotically, mechanically, or automatically regenerate. But, again, the definition of covenant of grace detailed and supported above excludes that erroneous take on the matter while preparing the ground for my (and Bavinck's) claim.

A good man might still well say, "OK, I see that God's covenant of grace is historical not ideological, corporate not strictly individual, relational not simply legal, and eschatological in that it concerns seed. But how can I be sure that God's covenant promise concerns the children of my household such that when I enter into this covenant my children do too?" One response to this well-received question is to say that all of God's covenantal dealings with man in the covenant of grace include their children. The chief example is Abraham.

God covenanted the following to Abraham: "And I will establish my covenant between me and thee and thy seed after thee in their generations for an everlasting covenant, to be a God unto thee, and to thy seed after thee" (Gen. 17:7). This covenant is not superficial, physical, or sub-salvific in nature. God covenants *to be God to Abraham's children*. God immediately adds the following words to Abraham, "Every man child among you shall be circumcised. And ye shall circumcise the flesh of your foreskin; and it shall be a token of the covenant betwixt me and you" (Gen. 17:10-11).

God told Abraham that he would be God to his children. And he told him to give those children the sign of that covenant. They were signed and sealed members of the covenant that God made with Abraham. And that covenant promised that God would be God to them. Now these covenant children of Abraham would have to follow in the footsteps of their father. They must keep covenant and the covenant has always been kept by faith. But they clearly grew up as insiders and not outsiders; they were marked with the covenant sign because they were covenant members and God said to them, "I am your God and you are my people." The same holds true for us today who are children of Abraham. The promises are to us and our children as they were to Abraham and his.

There is a common objection that arises at this point regarding what the Apostle Paul says in Romans 9:8, "They which are the children of the flesh, these are not the children of God: but the children of the promise are counted for seed." This text is taken by some to mean that a Christian cannot consider his own children as "children of the promise" as I've commended above. They may perhaps be only children of the flesh so it would be wrong to recognize them as children of the promise. But this false conclusion is corrected by the generational, concrete, and historical nature of God's covenant of grace. While it is true that one such as Ishmael eventually became a mere child of the flesh and was not counted as seed, he was, prior to being cast out, a child of the promise.[5] Recognizing him as such is not what made him so. Rather he was so and it was right to recognize him as such. Moreover, recognizing him as such was not presumption or a false recognition. He was recognized as a child of the promise as long as he was one. When he was cast out, he was recognized as merely a child of the flesh. Our job is not to attempt to determine the secret things and then live in light of them. Our job is to consider the things that have been revealed. The revealed things belong to us (Deut. 29:29).

It sounds strange to say that one could be a child of the promise and then become in the end merely a child of the flesh. But that concept is only strange so long as we maintain that child of the promise means nothing but elect or regenerate. There is a strict way to take the term or, in other words, a way of considering who will be children of the promise in the end. But more is going on when Paul speaks of children of the promise. John Calvin is very helpful here. He writes,

> [t]wo things are to be here considered. The first is, the promise of salvation given to Abraham belongs to all who can trace their natural descent to him; for it is offered to

---

5. Relatedly, the categories of "child of the flesh" and "child of the promise" are not abstract and watertight categories like "reprobate" and "elect." One can never be both "reprobate" and "elect" as he could be both a "child of the flesh" and a "child of the promise." Likewise, one could never cease to be "elect" or "reprobate" as one can cease to be a "child of the promise."

all without exception, and for this reason they are rightly called the heirs of the covenant made with Abraham; and in this respect they are his successors, or, as Scripture calls them, the children of the promise. For since it was the Lord's will that his covenant should be sealed, no less in Ishmael and Esau, than in Isaac and Jacob, it appears that they were not wholly alienated from him; except, it may be, you make no account of the circumcision, which was conferred on them by God's command; but it cannot be so regarded without dishonour to God. . . . The second point to be considered is, That the children of the promise are strictly those in whom its power and effect are found. On this account Paul denies here that all the children of Abraham were the children of God, though a covenant had been made with them by the Lord, for few continued in the faith of the covenant.[6]

In short, many evangelicals resonate with Calvin's second point above. But they have not given consideration to the first point he makes regarding the covenantal status of *natural children*. The restoration of the American family requires that we do so.

This chapter has demonstrated the nature of God's covenant with his bride. Furthermore, it has unearthed the organic relationship between God's covenant of grace and the covenant house. God's covenant of grace is not merely made with individuals. Rather, when God calls a man

---

6. John Calvin and John Owen, *Commentary on the Epistle of Paul the Apostle to the Romans* (Bellingham, WA: Logos Bible Software, 2010), 344–45.

to himself, his household comes with him into covenant with God. If a man grasps the marriage covenant in the last chapter, then he will rightly see the God-instituted family operating on earth. He will not be a mere individualist any longer. But, this man must go on to see that his family is related to God. The covenant house is not merely about the family operating as a unit. Headship is not merely about the husband having the final say as to whether the family moves to another state, buys a house, or sells a business. The covenant house is bound up in God's covenant with his people. God said to Abraham, "In thee shall all families of the earth be blessed" (Gen. 12:3).

Families, of course, include children. So the covenant household includes covenant children. As we will see in the next chapter, God has made glorious promises to these covenant children.

4 Covenant Children
A Heritage from the Lord

I n this chapter, I will cite several texts regarding God's promises to the Christian's children. But it is important to see that these promises come to us via covenant. They are covenant promises. In this sense, this chapter builds upon the previous ones. I should underscore this point. There is one approach to Christian childrearing that says, "The promises of God are *announced* to my children in a special way. They are *directed* to my children if my children would have them." This approach says, "My children can be on the team if they so choose. God commands them to join and welcomes them to join if they'd like." Then, there is a second approach to parenting which says, "The promise of grace in and by Christ is *upon* my children, sealed and covenanted to them and fulfilled by faith." This approach says, "My children are on the team and God's promises to the team are bound to them by covenant and kept by faith." I do not object to everything in the former. But I am advocating for the latter.

These covenantal promises will reorient our parenting. And we need to be reoriented. We have established that the family is in a bad way in our society. It has been hacked up ideologically for a long time. We are so far down the line that our legal system has gone over the cliff when it comes to the family. "You can't put toothpaste back in the tube" is a phrase that comes to mind. But so does, "with man it is impossible but with God all things are possible" (Matt. 10:26). This chapter will consider what covenant children are, what covenant promises God makes to them, and a common objection to the claim that the Christian's natural children are members of the New Covenant with its promises sealed to them. But before we get into the details, consider again just how far we have fallen.

In 1950 less than 5 percent of Americans were born out of wedlock. Back then such a child was called a bastard. People now view this term as a derogatory slur. But the word means that a particular child is illegitimate, born out of wedlock. Before the radical change in our legal system, the two basic categories regarding a child's status were legitimate and illegitimate. These categories are biblical, "If ye endure chastening, God dealeth with you as with sons; for what son is he whom the father chasteneth not? But if ye be without chastisement, whereof all are partakers, then are ye bastards, and not sons" (Heb. 12:7-8). So a legitimate child was one born in wedlock and an illegitimate child was one born out of wedlock. In Blackstone's *Commentaries on the Laws of England* we see that traditionally parents owed their legitimate children three particulars: maintenance, protection, and education, while an illegitimate child was only due maintenance.

So in 1950 less than 5 percent of American children were illegitimate. Today, that number has risen to 40 percent. Nearly half of the children in America are bastards. This statistic aligns with the dishonor we have brought upon marriage through no-fault divorce. Attorneys who practice family law deal with the devastating consequences of our legal system daily. Their work is like operating on a man with multiple sucking chest wounds after an incompetent surgeon went before you and hooked all of his insides up upside down. Our legal structure itself looks like something you would get after a tax-payer funded modern artist attempted to construct a city park playground after smoking whatever it is modern artists smoke. This familial disorder is downstream from our confusion regarding the covenantal status of our children and God's covenant promises to them.

The key thing that we have forgotten is that children are a heritage from the LORD. God says so through the wise King Solomon—"Lo, children are an heritage of the LORD: and the fruit of the womb is his reward" (Ps. 127:3). This text teaches that God himself gives children. There is a natural sense here which appears in other passages of Scripture. The Lord opens the womb, "And God remembered Rachel, and God hearkened to her, and opened her womb" (Gen. 30:22). The Lord knits man together in the womb, "For thou hast possessed my reins: thou hast covered me in my mother's womb. I will praise thee; for I am fearfully and wonderfully made" (Ps. 127:12-13). And the Lord brings forth from the womb, "Shall I bring to the birth, and not cause to bring forth? said the LORD: shall I cause to bring forth, and shut the womb? saith thy God" (Isa. 66:9). It is a comfort to know that the LORD, beginning, middle, and end, governs the begetting of children.

But more than simply the natural is going on when Solomon says, "children are an heritage of the LORD." Solomon is not only saying, "God gave you your children." God indeed gave you your children. Solomon wants us to know that much, but he wants us to know more than that. Children are not only a gift to us from the LORD: they are a *heritage* from the LORD. This word heritage carries the meaning of inheritance. When a father hands down an inheritance to his children, he is giving his children what belonged to him. Likewise, when the Father gives us children, he is giving us what belongs to him. The children are his. Now there is a sense in which this is true with unbelievers: the child in any womb is created in the image of God. But Solomon is speaking as king of Israel. When he speaks of the LORD, he speaks of the covenant-keeping God. The children are God's arrows in the hand of a mighty warrior (Ps. 127:4). So when Solomon says that children are a heritage from the LORD, he's not primarily speaking to a random child's status as a divine image-bearer. Rather, he is speaking to the covenant people of God about the LORD giving them his own heritage, covenant children.

Many American Christians have a place for dedicating their children to God. But they have not thought through the basis for such a dedication. Does God want them in any kind of special way? Will God accept them when you dedicate them to him or is there just a chance that he might accept them one day in the future if you dedicate them to him when they are babies? If God does accept them when you dedicate them to him as babies, what is their status before him at that time? Has God made promises to your children that are any different than the promises he makes generally to all men? These are the kinds of questions that are addressed by the covenant, and they are the kind of questions that atomized Americans struggle to answer.

We saw in the last chapter that Abraham's children were in covenant with God for they were a part of Abraham's household. The same was the case for Joshua, and the same is the case for New Testament saints today. The administration of this covenant of grace has changed, but the inclusion of one's children in the covenant of grace has not changed. The promise was to Abraham and his children in the Old and the promise is the same in the New, "Then Peter said unto them, Repent, and be baptized every one of you in the name of Jesus Christ for the remission of sins, and ye shall receive the gift of the Holy Ghost. For the promise is unto you, and to your children, and to all that are afar off, even as many as the Lord our God shall call" (Acts 2:38-39).

This covenantal understanding of the house explains the manner in which Paul and Silas preached the gospel to the Philippian jailer. Not only was the Philippian jailer a Gentile. But the apostle's gospel preaching was announced via the New Covenant. They said, "Believe on the Lord Jesus Christ, and thou shalt be saved, *and thy house*" (Acts 16:31). If you have been an evangelical for any length of time, then think about how strange that evangelistic message sounds. I have spent my whole life in faithful, gospel-preaching, evangelistic churches and communities (for which I am remarkably grateful). These communities and ministries have been marked by a burning desire to share the good news with a lost and dying world. It strikes me as odd that in all of that time, I have never heard a single evangelist preach to a man the way Paul and Silas preached to this Philippian jailer. Imagine a modern day gospel preacher, announcing good news to a room full of people, saying something like, "Jesus Christ lived, died, and rose again for sinners like you and me. Now every head bowed and every eye closed. We have come to the moment of decision. Here is the critical thing: Believe on the Lord Jesus Christ and you *and your house* will be saved."

Now it is important to see that Paul and Silas followed up this word to the Philippian jailer by speaking the word of the Lord to him and all that were in his house. Any idea that a covenant house will be just fine with the Lord without the members of that house hearing his word is folly.

That truth is the kind that most evangelicals know and ought not to forget. But the question that most evangelicals have not thought through is, "Why in the world would Paul and Silas tell the Philippian jailer, 'Believe on the Lord Jesus Christ and you will be saved, and your house?'" The answer is, Paul and Silas knew that they were speaking to a covenant head of a covenant family. They knew that when the Philippian jailer believed on the Lord, he could say what Joshua said years before, "As for me and my house, we will serve the Lord." Paul and Silas recalled what God had promised to Abraham many years prior, "In you shall all the families of the earth be blessed" (Gen. 12:3).

Imagine a great king, a king of kings. This king conquers another king such that the latter king is now subject to the conquering king. Do you think that the conquering king says, "You, conquered king, will now be my loyal subject, but your kingdom can remain outside of my jurisdiction?" That is not how things work. The conquered king is now the loyal subject of the conquering king, and the whole kingdom of the conquered king is now the loyal subject of the conquering king as well.

It follows that when a father sits down at the table to lead his family in family worship, he has the right and duty to pray, 'God *our* Father," and all of his children (the one-, two-, and three-year-old not excluded) are represented in that word "our." This father has the right and duty to pray, "We thank you Christ for being our Savior," and his children are included in that "our." This father has the right and duty to pray, "We praise you Holy Spirit, our

Comforter," and his whole household is included in that "our." The household is included because the household is in covenant with God, not just the father.

Modern evangelicals hear this and think, "But how can the father say that? Those little kids have not professed faith." The answer is that he can pray that way because God has brought him and his household into the covenant of grace. And so he can say with Joshua, "As for me and my house, we will serve the Lord."

I am well aware of the confusion associated with the covenant idea. Many Christians are just not sure how their family covenant is bound up in God's covenant of grace with his people. They do not think of God's covenant of grace in terms of a house, or a covenant, or an earthly organization with members and non-members. Thus they look at their young children, whom they love dearly, and they hope they are genuinely trusting the Lord (i.e. eating the ice cream from the illustration in the last chapter). But in an effort not to presume upon God, they cannot say to their young children plainly, "God is *our God*, yours and mine. Jesus died *for us*, you and me. Christ is *our High Priest*, you and me."

The best one can say with no covenant (no ice cream shop) is God will be your God if you believe. Christ will be yours if you believe. Now hopefully that sounds just right to you, because it is right. Covenantal parents can and do say the same thing to their children. And they say more. They say, "God is our God. He has promised to be so. He has promised us grace in and by Jesus Christ."

We see God's promise of grace to us and our children in many places. Here are a few:

God says to Abraham, "And I will establish my covenant between me and you and your offspring after you throughout their generations for an everlasting covenant, to be God to you and to your offspring after you" (Gen. 17:7). Some would say that "offspring" in this text only refers to Jesus Christ, not to Abraham's offspring. And Galatians 3:16 ought to be carefully considered for Paul says, "Now to Abraham and his seed were the promises made. He saith not, And to seeds, as of many; but as of one, And to thy seed, which is Christ." It is true that the "seed" in Genesis 17:7 is singular. But it does not follow that *only* Christ is in view. Christ is in view, and so are Abraham's children. We can see that in the very verse in question. God says in Genesis 17:7 that he will be God to Abraham and to his offspring after him in *their* generations. And that *their* is plural. Christians, who are children of Abraham, trust God in this same way. He has promised to be God to us and to our offspring after us in their generations.

We see the same grace of God in the prophet Jeremiah when God says, "I will give them one heart and one way, that they may fear me forever, for their own good and the good of their children after them" (Jer. 32:39). This text is especially important for it speaks to the New Covenant, the new administration of the covenant of grace. This New Covenant, like the covenant of grace in the old, includes the good of our children for the children of God's covenant people are included in his covenant.

The prophet Isaiah signals the same thing. God says,

> And as for me, this is my covenant with them, says the Lord: "My Spirit that is upon you, and my words that I have put in your mouth, shall not depart out of your mouth, or out of the mouth of your offspring, or out of the mouth of your children's offspring" says the Lord, "from this time forth and forevermore." (Isa. 59:21)

There is no ambiguity in this text. God clearly refers to covenant here. He says that this covenant includes his very Spirit being upon the children of his people, and their children's children. Not only God's Spirit, but God covenants to put his word in the mouth of our children and children's children.

God strikes this same note through King David, "But the steadfast love of the Lord is from everlasting to everlasting on those who fear him, and his righteousness to children's children, to those who keep his covenant and remember to do his commandments" (Ps. 103:17-18). Again, we see the covenant resulting in blessing upon children and children's children. Particularly in these verses, the very righteousness of the Lord is upon the grandchildren of covenant keepers.

God speaks a similar promise through the prophet Isaiah, "They shall not build, and another inhabit; they shall not plant, and another eat: for as the days of a tree are the days of my people, and mine elect shall long enjoy the work of their hands. They shall not labour in vain, nor bring forth for trouble; for they are the seed of the blessed of the LORD, and their offspring with them" (Isa. 65:22-23). God makes specific promises here regarding "offspring." And he makes this promise regarding offspring to a people that he calls "my people." The nature of that promise is that God's people will not beget children in vain or bring them forth for trouble.

John Calvin, speaking of the blessing of God in this verse, says,

> For whence come fears and terrors, whence come alarms, but from the curse of God? When the curse has been removed, the Prophet therefore says justly that parents, together with their offspring, shall be free from dread and anxious solicitude; because they shall be convinced that they shall always be safe and sound through the favour of God.[1]

Many parents are not free of this dread. They are given to the anxiety that Calvin says parents and children can be free from. What can happen in some cases is that the parents begin to think that anxiety and dread is what keeps them faithful parents. Their parental work is driven by the anxiety such that encouragement to be rid of the anxiety sounds to them like an encouragement to presume upon God for the welfare of their children. But the point is not to be a presumptuous parent, thinking God

---

1. John Calvin and William Pringle, *Commentary on the Book of the Prophet Isaiah*, vol. 4 (Bellingham, WA: Logos Bible Software, 2010), 403.

will bless your children apart from faith and work. The point is to trust God and his promises. God has lavished them upon us.

He says through the prophet Isaiah, "For as the new heavens and the new earth that I make shall remain before me, says the Lord, so shall your offspring and your name remain" (Isa. 66:22). God speaks here again of generational blessing. The offspring of God's covenant people will remain before him. This promise surely includes the church of God which Christ himself builds. And it surely includes the offspring of the covenant people.

We see this same promise in Psalm 102:28 as the psalmist says to God, "The children of your servants shall dwell secure; their offspring shall be established before you" (Ps. 102:28). This word is spoken to God. So the servants in view are servants of God, and those servants are promised that their children will dwell secure and be established before the Lord.

The several texts cited above speak of God's gracious promise to our children. As I mentioned at the outset of this chapter, these are covenant promises to covenant children, children of the promise. I have claimed that these covenant promises were not merely for the children of saints in the Old Testament, but they carry over to children of the saints in the New as well. That claim is well suited to the view which holds there is but one covenant of grace differently administered. If Abraham's children were in, then our children are in too for we are in the same covenant for substance. But there are objections.

While there is not space to answer every objection, I will address what appears to be the strongest one.

AN OBJECTION TO NEW COVENANT PROMISES FOR CHILDREN

One objection claims that the New Covenant is so new that natural children are not included in it like they were in the Old. This argument holds that there was a genealogical principle in the Abrahamic covenant that does not carry over to the New Covenant. The chief text of Scripture supplied as support for this claim is Jeremiah 31:31-34. God says through the prophet—

> Behold, the days come, saith the Lord, That I will make a new covenant with the house of Israel, and with the house of Judah: Not according to the covenant that I made with their fathers In the day that I took them by the hand To bring them out of the land of Egypt; Which my covenant they brake, Although I was an husband unto them, saith the Lord: But this shall be the covenant that I will make with the house of Israel; After those days, saith the Lord, I will put my law in their inward parts, And write it in their hearts; And will be their God, And they shall be my people. And they shall teach no more every man his neighbour, and every man his brother, saying, Know the Lord: For they shall all know me, From the least of them unto the greatest of them, saith the Lord: For I will forgive their iniquity, And I will remember their sin no more.

The argument then runs as follows. The Old Covenant which God made with Abraham and Israel included natural children and Israel broke that covenant. The New Covenant will be different in that it is not made with natural children but spiritual children (only those who are regenerated unto saving faith) and thus it will not be broken as the Old. Moreover, there will be no need for every man to tell his brother to know the LORD for each and every one in this New Covenant is regenerated unto saving faith. There are no unregenerate covenant members in the New Covenant as there was in the Old.

Not only can I see how someone could hold to this line of thinking, I myself did hold to it for some time albeit with a variety of modifications, clarifications, and attendant arguments. Indeed for me this whole book is an exercise in what Chesterton once said:

> If this book is a joke it is a joke against me. I am the man who with the utmost daring discovered what had been discovered before. . . . No one can think my case more ludicrous than I think it myself; no reader can accuse me here of trying to make a fool of him: I am the fool of this story, and no rebel shall hurl me from my throne.[2]

Indeed for some time, I considered the various biblical promises noted above as promises God made to Israel and their offspring and *in some general sense* similar promises

---

2. G. K. Chesterton, *Orthodoxy* (Chicago, IL: Moody Publishers, 2009), 23.

were made to New Covenant members and their offspring. I could not say with confidence that they were *covenant promises from God to covenant children in the New Covenant* for I was convinced that New Covenant membership necessitated regeneration. I was not prepared to claim the active regeneration of my infant so I was not ready to recognize either their New Covenant membership nor the biblical promises above as being vouchsafed to them by Christ's blood. I took these promises as announced to the Christian's children, even promises made to such children in a special way given their presence in a Christian home. But I did not take them as promises stuck to them, promises from God signed and sealed upon them. But that is what they are. They are not promises potentially made to your seed or promises merely announced like a general gospel call to the world. They are promises covenantally made, indeed, promises vouchsafed to your children by the blood of Christ. They are sworn oaths of blessing made to your children in a particular way for they are covenant children and the promises are to them, and fulfilled by faith.

But what about the Jeremiah 31 objection above? I believe the objection I detailed above simply straps too much on the back of Jeremiah 31:31-34. He is a strong prophet, but if we load the stated objection on his shoulders, then we weigh him down with more of an argument than he can bear. Really, we must take it easier on him. The objection claims that Jeremiah 31 proves that each and every New Covenant member is regenerate when Jeremiah's point is that the New Covenant will be better than the Old. Particularly, the New Covenant will be better in that it will not be broken as the Old was, it consists of God's law being written on the heart of his covenant people, and it will be far more efficacious and potent in the lives of the covenant people.

Regarding the New Covenant not being broken, Jeremiah's point is not that an individual covenant member cannot break covenant with God in the New Covenant. Rather, his point is that the New Covenant itself will not be broken. The Old Covenant as a whole was broken such that it came to an end (2 Cor. 3:11). In other words, Jeremiah is not saying that a man cannot walk out of the New Covenant ice cream shop. He is saying that the New Covenant ice cream shop is never fading away like the old form of the shop did.

Concerning God's law written on the heart in the New Covenant, Jeremiah speaks to the degree of the Spirit's power and efficaciousness upon the New Covenant people. He does not imply that the saints under the old administration of the covenant of grace were saved without the work of the Spirit upon the heart. Calvin, for example, writes, "A question may however be here moved, Was the grace of regeneration wanting to the Fathers under the Law? But this is quite preposterous."[3] He places the difference not as to the substance of the Spirit, but the form or degree of the Spirit—"Then we know that this grace

---

3. John Calvin and John Owen, *Commentaries on the Prophet Jeremiah and the Lamentations*, vol. 4 (Bellingham, WA: Logos Bible Software, 2010), 131.

of God was rare and little known under the Law; but that under the Gospel the gifts of the Spirit have been more abundantly poured forth, and that God has dealt more bountifully with his Church."[4]

Calvin tracks with this distinction between substance and form throughout his exegesis:

> He afterwards says, *I will put my Law in their inward parts.* By these words he confirms what we have said, that the newness, which he before mentioned, was not so as to the substance, but as to the form only: for God does not say here, "I will give you another Law," but *I will write my Law,* that is, the same Law, which had formerly been delivered to the Fathers. He then does not promise anything different as to the essence of the doctrine, but he makes the difference to be in the form only.[5]

In other words, whether you believe there is one ice cream shop in substance which has undergone a significant renovation in form and structure with the coming of Christ, or you believe there has been two separate ice cream shops, the old housing the natural family and the new merely regenerate individuals, makes a big difference.

The greater efficaciousness and potency of the New Covenant is seen in Jeremiah's language—"they shall teach no more every man his neighbour, and every man his brother, saying, 'Know the Lord'" (Jer. 31:34). Jeremiah

4. Ibid., 131.
5. Ibid., 131–32.

here speaks hyperbolically. His point is not that the substance of the New Covenant is different such that each and every New Covenant member is regenerate, opposed to the Old when that was not the case. Rather, Jeremiah amplifies the point that the New Covenant manifests God and his truth far more brightly than the Old. Again, Calvin writes,

> Here is mentioned another difference between the old and the new covenant, even that God, who had obscurely manifested himself under the Law, would send forth a fuller light, so that the knowledge of him would be commonly enjoyed. But he hyperbolically extols this favour, when he says that no one would have need of a teacher or instructor, as every one would have himself sufficient knowledge. We therefore consider that the object of the Prophet is mainly to shew, that so great would be the light of the Gospel, that it would be clearly evident, that God under it deals more bountifully with his people, because its truth shines forth as the sun at noon-day.[6]

Indeed, God deals more bountifully with his covenant people in the New Covenant, not less bountifully. The fact that God told Abraham to place the sign of the covenant upon his children is a testimony that his children were included in God's covenant with him. Does it not stand to reason that in the more bountiful covenant, the children would likewise be included? If we would see

6. Ibid., 134.

the family restored, then it must be restored on a sure foundation, not a potential one. Those covenant promises upon which we build are yes and amen in Christ, and those blood bought blessings are upon the whole household from the greatest of them to the least.

5 Covenant Kingdom
Let the Children Come to Me

Wе started in chapter 1 with the troubling truth that legally speaking our children do not belong to us anymore. This legal development is downstream from an a-covenantal approach to the family that evangelicals have imbibed far and wide. If we would rectify our ongoing legal and cultural train wreck, then we must recover the covenantal household. Chapter 2 addressed covenant marriage which stands at the center of the covenant household and covenant children. Chapter 3 demonstrated that marriage between one man and one woman is not the only covenant marriage that exists. Human marriage testifies to another very real marriage, the marriage between Christ and his bride, the church. Both of these covenants are more real than modern man thinks. There are clear parties involved, clear promises and stipulations, real bonds established, and an organic relationship between the two. Chapter 4 surveyed various covenant promises regarding covenant children, further establishing that the Christian's covenant children are included among God's covenant people, the bride of Christ.

We now need to consider the implications for the covenant household. Take a normal family, let's call them the Robertsons. We have a real marriage between Mr. and Mrs. Robertson, and we have three Robertson children. This family is a Christian home, a covenant household. The Robertsons go to church on Sunday. The Robertsons worship the Triune God. The littlest of the Robertsons are included in this covenant household which is related to God covenantally. The question now is, "What relationship does this covenant household have to the house and kingdom of God?"

The Westminster Confession of Faith says,

> The visible church, which is also catholic or universal under the gospel (not confined to one nation, as before under the law), consists of all those throughout the world that profess the true religion; and of their children: and is the kingdom of the Lord Jesus Christ, the house and family of God, out of which there is no ordinary possibility of salvation. (WCF 25:2)

The visible church is called "the kingdom of the Lord Jesus Christ." The children of those who profess the true religion are in that visible church. These children are in the kingdom of the Lord Jesus Christ and this particular kingdom is *visible*.

I recall growing up in the church singing an old Gaither hymn called "The Family of God." In that catchy chorus we sang,

> I'm so glad I'm a part
> Of the family of God
> I've been washed in the fountain
> Cleansed by His blood
> Joint heirs with Jesus
> As we travel this sod
> For I'm part of the family,
> The family of God.[1]

Now I was gathered with my family as I sang this song. I was gathered with God's people, and even as a young child, I did not conflate these two families. I knew that my earthly "father's house" was not identical to my heavenly father's house. But, at the same time, I was very much aware that these two houses were intimately related and organically connected.

Herman Bavinck provides some foundational support for the topic at hand and this foundation is lost on many atomized Americans:

> Humanity is not an aggregate of individuals but an organic unity, one race, one family. Angels, on the other hand, all stand side-by-side, independently of one another. They

1. Bill and Gloria Gaither, "The Family of God," 1970.

were all created at the same time and are not the products of procreation. Among them a divine judgment such as was pronounced upon all humanity in Adam would not have been possible: everyone stood or fell on his own. But that is not how it is among us. God created all of us from one man (Acts 17: 26); we are not a heap of souls piled on a piece of ground, but all blood relatives of one another, connected to one another by a host of ties, therefore conditioning one another and being conditioned by one another.[2]

Now the headship of our Father Adam is unique. He was head of the entire human race. He was set up by God as a representative of the human race in the covenant of life in the Garden. No earthly father stands in the place of Adam for his posterity for the covenant of life has been broken, the curse of that covenant rendered down upon us such that none of us are getting past those cherubim with flaming sword (Gen. 3:24).

The household is, however, still a covenant household. As Bavinck says above, the family is an organic unity, not a heap of souls piled. Humanity itself is connected by a host of ties. And how much more the covenant household flowing from God's work of covenant marriage in which he joins man and woman together?

The Westminster Confession holds this covenant house to be of such significance that children of those who profess the true religion are themselves reckoned members of the house, family, and even kingdom of God.

2. Bavinck, *Reformed Dogmatics*, 3:102.

Matthew 19:13-15 supports this claim, and it should be understood in light of the various texts considered in chapter 4 regarding the Christian's children. Matthew's gospel says, "Then were there brought unto him little children, that he should put his hands on them, and pray: and the disciples rebuked them. But Jesus said, Suffer little children, and forbid them not, to come unto me: for of such is the kingdom of heaven. And he laid his hands on them, and departed thence."

Trusted Reformed commentators from the past have said things of this text that cause modern evangelicals no little confusion. Calvin, for example, says of this text:

> To exclude from the grace of redemption those who are of that age would be too cruel; and therefore it is not without reason that we employ this passage as a shield against the Anabaptists. They refuse baptism to infants, because infants are incapable of understanding that mystery which is denoted by it. We, on the other hand, maintain that, since baptism is the pledge and figure of the forgiveness of sins, and likewise of adoption by God, it ought not to be denied to infants, whom God adopts and washes with the blood of his Son.[3]

Some teach that Christ was merely illustrating that the child-like are of the kingdom, but not the children of the Christians themselves. But Calvin, along with the

3. John Calvin and William Pringle, *Commentary on a Harmony of the Evangelists Matthew, Mark, and Luke*, vol. 2 (Bellingham, WA: Logos Bible Software, 2010), 390–391.

Westminster Divines, sees more going on in Christ's lay-
ing on of hands and praying in this passage:

> Certainly, the *laying on of hands* was not a trifling or empty
> sign, and the prayers of Christ were not idly wasted in
> air. But he could not present the infants solemnly to God
> without giving them purity. And for what did he pray for
> them, but that they might be received into the number of
> the children of God?[4]

Along these lines, the kingdom of the Lord Jesus
Christ is not merely something that is *oriented* to covenant
children. Christ's kingdom is not simply promised them.
Praise God that it is. Praise God that the promises are to
us and to our children. But Calvin and Westminster say
more. The kingdom of God *consists* of these covenant children. Covenant children are in the family and kingdom of
the Lord Jesus Christ.

Indeed, Calvin insists that these children are among
Christ's flock—

> In short, by embracing them, he testified that they were
> reckoned by Christ among his flock. And if they were
> partakers of the spiritual gifts, which are represented by
> Baptism, it is unreasonable that they should be deprived
> of the outward sign. But it is presumption and sacrilege
> to drive far from the fold of Christ those whom he cher-
> ishes in his bosom, and to shut the door, and exclude as

4. Ibid.

strangers those whom he does not wish to be forbidden to come to him.[5]

YOU MUST BE BORN AGAIN

After reading Calvin, the evangelical rightly raises his hand and says, "But except a man be born again, he cannot see the kingdom of God." That is exactly right and precisely what our Lord says in John 3:3. He adds, "Except a man be born of water and of the Spirit, he cannot enter the kingdom of God" (John 3:5). This truth must be clearly and whole-heartedly affirmed. Unless a man be born again, he cannot see the kingdom of God. Unless a man be born of the Spirit, he cannot enter the kingdom of God.

We must affirm that point while also affirming what Calvin says above. We affirm that a man must be born again to enter into the kingdom while maintaining what Christ said to his disciples who rebuked those who brought little children to him: "Suffer the little children to come unto me, and forbid them not: for of such is the kingdom of God" (Mark 10:14).

Remember that the Westminster Confession states that the visible church is the kingdom of God. A key text in support of this conclusion is Matthew 16:18-19. There Christ says to Peter,

> Blessed art thou, Simon Barjona: for flesh and blood hath not revealed it unto thee, but my Father which is in heaven.

5. Ibid.

> And I say also unto thee, That thou art Peter, and upon this rock I will build my church; and the gates of hell shall not prevail against it. And I will give unto thee the keys of the kingdom of heaven: and whatsoever thou shalt bind on earth shall be bound in heaven: and whatsoever thou shalt loose on earth shall be loosed in heaven.

This text teaches that the kingdom of heaven in some fashion exists on earth. Indeed the government of this kingdom down here is acknowledged by heaven.[6] This passage undergirds the claim that the kingdom of God can be spoken of as the church and vice versa. According to Geerhardus Vos, the church-form of the kingdom is a supernatural link between the present life and the life of eternity. Indeed, "the church actually has within herself the powers of the world to come.[7]

Vos considers the kingdom of God with regard to the invisible and visible church. Concerning the invisible church, Vos writes,

> So far as extent of membership is concerned, Jesus plainly leads us to identify the invisible church and the kingdom.

---

6. In reference to this text, Geerhardus Vos says, "The kingdom of heaven appears as something existing, in part at least, on earth. Peter receives the keys of the kingdom to bind or loose on earth. What he does in the administration of the kingdom here below will be recognized in heaven." Geerhardus Vos, *The Teaching of Jesus Concerning the Kingdom of God and the Church*, ed. John H. Kerr, Second Edition, Revised (New York: American Tract Society, 1903), 149.

7. Ibid., 156.

It is impossible to be in the one without being in the other. We have our Lord's explicit declaration in John 3:3, 5, to the effect that nothing less than the new birth can enable man to see the kingdom or enter into it. The kingdom, therefore, as truly as the invisible church is constituted by the regenerate; the regenerate alone experience in themselves its power, cultivate its righteousness, enjoy its blessings.[8]

Upon upholding the necessity of the new birth, Vos proceeds to ask,

But what about the relation of the visible church to the kingdom? Here again we must first of all insist upon it, that our Lord looked upon the visible church as a veritable embodiment of his kingdom. Precisely because the invisible church realizes the kingship of God, the visible church must likewise partake of this character.[9]

Vos adds, "In Matthew 13:41 the kingdom of the Son of man, out of which the angels in the last day will remove all things that cause stumbling and them that do iniquity, is nothing else but the visible church."[10] Refusing to divorce the kingdom from life in this world, Vos states, "We must say, therefore, that the kingdom-forces which are at work, the kingdom-life which exists in the invisible

8. Ibid., 159.
9. Ibid., 161.
10. Ibid.

sphere, find expression in the kingdom-organism of the visible church.[11]

The payoff of Vos's analysis is that membership in the visible church involves membership in the veritable embodiment of Christ's kingdom, while at the same time one must be born again if he is to experience in himself the power, righteousness and blessings of that kingdom. Some would downplay the significance of kingdom, covenant, and church inclusion, seeing that a man can fall away from such inclusion. But downplaying covenant, visible church, and kingdom membership in that way is unwise. Consider the beauty of covenant and church membership:

> As a promissory covenant its total content is brought into contact with the individual already as an infant. When that infant later enters into covenantal consciousness by active faith, this faith sums up all that is included in the covenant, so that the wide, rich world of God's works of grace is opened up to his sight, a perspective looking backwards and forward. It is just this beautiful outlook which leads one to call the idea of the covenant of grace a "mother-idea." The covenant is a mother because it spiritually bears sons and daughters by the power of divine grace and the promises, a mother because its children have received everything from it, because it has given birth to them, sustains them, feeds, and blesses them.

11. Ibid., 162.

Reformed theology has certainly realized that the church has two sides, and that besides being the assembly of believers and the revelation of the body of Christ, she must also be the means by which new believers are added. But it has not separated these two sides; rather it has kept them in organic connection. Just because the promises of God have been given to the assembly of believers, in its entirety, including their seed, this assembly is also a mother who conceives sons and daughters and is made to rejoice in her children by the Lord. The name "mother" signifies this truly Reformed point of view in distinction from other terms such as "institution of salvation."[12]

Vos is glorious here: "As a promissory covenant, its total content is brought into contact with the individual already as an infant." But he rightly maintains that this infant enters into "covenantal consciousness" by "active faith." Moreover, not only must you be born again to enter the kingdom, but "the covenant is a mother because it spiritually bears sons and daughters by the power of divine grace." In other words, the covenant child, even as an infant, is genuinely in the covenant of grace and in the visible church. Must there be an "active faith" in such an individual if heaven is to be obtained? Absolutely! Must such a child be born again if he is to experience within himself the power of the kingdom of heaven? Indeed,

12. Geerhardus Vos, *Redemptive History and Biblical Interpretation: The Shorter Writings of Geerhardus Vos*, ed. Richard B. Gaffin Jr. (Phillipsburg, NJ: P&R Publishing, 2001), 262–63.

and that birth comes of the Spirit, ordinarily through the church and her ministry.

The point of this chapter may be one of the hardest for many readers to grasp. But it is a critical point, especially for Christian parents who must bring their children up "in the nurture and admonition of the Lord" (Eph. 6:4). Notice, the nurture and admonition of the Lord is not merely the doctrine with which we instruct the child. Our call is not simply to teach our children the Bible like we teach our children mathematics and the basic rules of grammar. We should do that much, of course. But the text says to bring them up *in something*, namely the nurture and admonition of the Lord. The point of this chapter regarding their location in the covenant, church, and kingdom is related to the fulfillment of that imperative.

Many evangelicals think of membership in the covenant, church, and kingdom as a membership that one experiences strictly by personal decision. Children are conceived of as outside of God's covenant, church, and kingdom until they make a personal decision, at which point they become members of the covenant, church, and kingdom. Depending on the tradition, some would say the child can never fall away from this membership and others say that the child can fall away from the covenant, church, and kingdom. The commonly held idea in both, however, is that the child is outside until he makes a personal decision. Thus the covenant as a "mother-idea" is lost.

But older Reformed authors thought differently. You find them speaking of God's gracious covenant with

Adam after his fall in such a way that his seed are included in that covenant and the church. The English theologians John Owen and John Ball for example, speak of Cain as a member of the church before he murdered his brother Abel.[13] Cain's membership was not the result of a decision he made at an age of accountability. It was a result of the covenant of grace God made with his father after his fall.

Speaking of this covenant, John Ball writes,

> Under this covenant outwardly administered, were comprehended both *Adam* and his posterity, even so many as he should dedicate unto God, or should accept of the Covenant, until by willful departure from the faith and worship of God they discovenanted themselves, and their posterity. As the Covenant was after made with *Abraham* and his seed, and is now made with believing Parents for themselves and their children after them: so was it with *Adam*, and those that should descend from his loins.[14]

Ball employs a common distinction with the words "covenant outwardly administered." This distinction between the covenant administered internally and externally is often utilized and begins to make sense as one grasps the nature of a covenant as described previously

---

13. John Owen, *Biblical Theology* (Morgan, PA: Soli Deo Gloria Publications, 1996), 184, 188.
14. John Ball, *A Treatise of the Covenant of Grace* (London: Forgotten Books, 2018), 45.

in chapter 3. Someone might ask however, "What good is a covenant outwardly administered if a man might 'discovenant' himself and fall away?" Along these lines, Paul asks, "What advantage then hath the Jew? or what profit is there of circumcision? Much every way: chiefly, because that unto them were committed the oracles of God" (Rom. 3:1-2). What advantage has the child who finds himself in the covenant of grace, the visible church, and the kingdom of God? Much advantage.

There is a bit of a paradigm shift here for many people. So here are three passages that shed light on the idea. Jesus says in John 15:5—

I am the true vine, and my Father is the husbandman. Every branch in me that beareth not fruit he taketh away: and every branch that beareth fruit, he purgeth it, that it may bring forth more fruit. Now ye are clean through the word which I have spoken unto you. Abide in me, and I in you. As the branch cannot bear fruit of itself, except it abide in the vine; no more can ye, except ye abide in me. I am the vine, ye are the branches: He that abideth in me, and I in him, the same bringeth forth much fruit: for without me ye can do nothing. If a man abide not in me, he is cast forth as a branch, and is withered; and men gather them, and cast them into the fire, and they are burned.

Jesus says that there are branches in him that can be taken away. Branches are really in him and they are truly taken away and cast forth to be burned in fire. An Arminian would point to this text as support for his position that a born again believer in the Lord Jesus Christ can fall away. A Calvinist insists that the branch in question, which was "in Christ," was not a born again believer, and he is right about that. But, the question follows, "Was that branch genuinely in Christ?" Or in other words, "Was that branch in Christ covenantally? Was that branch in the church and kingdom of the Lord Jesus?" The answer is, yes.

The Apostle Paul communicates this same idea in Romans 11:17-21 when he writes—

> And if some of the branches be broken off, and thou, being a wild olive tree, wert grafted in among them, and with them partakest of the root and fatness of the olive tree; Boast not against the branches. But if thou boast, thou bearest not the root, but the root thee. Thou wilt say then, The branches were broken off, that I might be grafted in. Well; because of unbelief they were broken off, and thou standest by faith. Be not highminded, but fear: For if God spared not the natural branches, take heed lest he also spare not thee.

Here again branches that were genuinely a part of the olive tree were "broken off." And why were they broken off? Because of unbelief. Others were grafted in, and how do they stand? How do they remain in the olive tree? "By faith." The warning is clear. If those grafted in are highminded and unbelieving, they too will not be spared by

God but broken off. The same covenantal logic applies here as it does in John 15.

Hebrews 10:29 communicates the same principle when it says, "Of how much sorer punishment, suppose ye, shall he be thought worthy, who hath trodden under foot the Son of God, and hath counted the blood of the covenant, wherewith he was sanctified, an unholy thing, and hath done despite unto the Spirit of grace?" In context, the author is writing to "brethren" (v. 19). And he warns them about sinning willfully after receiving a knowledge of the truth (v. 26). The people in question will suffer a sorer punishment than those who despised Moses and "died without mercy" (v. 28). The people in question were sanctified by the blood of the covenant. That word "sanctified" carries the meaning of including a person in the inner circle of what is holy. In other words, such a one has been included in the covenant of grace, the visible church and kingdom of the Lord Jesus Christ. Such a man is like a bad fish that was genuinely in the kingdom of heaven, but will be cast away in the end— "Again, the kingdom of heaven is like unto a net, that was cast into the sea, and gathered of every kind: Which, when it was full, they drew to shore, and sat down, and gathered the good into vessels, but cast the bad away" (Matt. 13:47-48).

The covenant household does not live in isolation. Remember, chapter 1 lamented the loss of the covenant household. Chapter 2 considered marriage as the foundation of a covenant household. Chapter 3 demonstrated that the covenant household is linked up to God and his gracious covenant. Chapter 4 testified that covenant children too are members of the covenant household and the covenant of grace, and here chapter 5 shows that this covenant household is a part of the kingdom of God. The families of the earth indeed are blessed (Gen. 12:3), and they are blessed by being joined together in God's church and kingdom.

When a man grasps God's covenant of grace and the covenant house, he will find that his heart has been enlarged. He will find an unexpected manifestation of Jesus' promise in Mark 10:29-30,

> Verily I say unto you, There is no man that hath left house, or brethren, or sisters, or father, or mother, or wife, or children, or lands, for my sake, and the gospel's, But he shall receive an hundredfold now in this time, houses, and brethren, and sisters, and mothers, and children, and lands, with persecutions; and in the world to come eternal life.

The payoff for the little ones is not insignificant. We not only take our little ones to church. Our little ones are members of the church. Paul says, "We who are many are one bread," (1 Cor. 10:17), and our children are bread. The covenant house employs the plural "we," saying, "We are no more strangers and foreigners, but fellow citizens with the saints, and of the household of God" (Eph. 2:19). If the littlest child in the home asks, "Mom, am I with you being built on the foundation of the apostles and the prophets?" Mom cheerfully looks the little one in the eyes and says, "Indeed you are, my dear." And when another little one asks, "Dad, am I grafted in the olive tree? Am I being framed together with you unto a holy temple in the Lord?" Dad replies with joy, "You are, my son, and our God and Father is faithful to his covenant. Trust him now and always for every one of his promises are yes and amen in Christ . . . and he is our chief cornerstone" (Eph. 2:20).

6 Covenant Education
Raise Them in the Lord

I mentioned in the introduction of this book that it would not be justifiably classified as a "how-to read." I'm all for putting feet to pavement. But that process does begin with knowing where the pavement is. We have been in discovery mode. I have aimed to unearth the nature of the covenant household, and in so doing to signal a new direction down an old path. This goal has involved identifying how we got lost in these woods in the first place (chapter 1), the nature of covenant marriage (chapter 2), the covenant of grace (chapter 3), covenant children (chapter 4), and the kingdom of God (chapter 5). In this chapter, I aim to describe covenant education. In one sense, this chapter may appear to be more practical. But, I should forewarn you that I'm still after the exposing of an ancient way more than I am after the way you stride down it, and one of the key elements of this old path is covenant nurture or education.

The intention of this chapter is not only to affirm that the ministry of education indeed belongs to the family, not the state or the church. Additionally, I hope to lay some groundwork toward a covenantal vision for the education of children. You only need to look around for a moment to see that, in the United States, we have completely abdicated the education of our children to the state. Approximately ninety percent of children in America go to government schools. Those government schools forbid the public profession and worship of the Lord Jesus Christ, whose name is *the truth*, and they look as prosperous as Hiroshima did in September of 1945.

Several texts of Scripture signal that the family, not the state, is the sphere responsible for the education of children. Deuteronomy 6:6-9 says—

> And these words, which I command thee this day, shall be in thine heart: And thou shalt teach them diligently unto thy children, and shalt talk of them when thou sittest in thine house, and when thou walkest by the way, and when thou liest down, and when thou risest up. And thou shalt bind them for a sign upon thine hand, and they shall be as frontlets between thine eyes. And thou shalt write them upon the posts of thy house, and on thy gates.

I will note here in passing that many Christians hear this text and assume that merely a portion of their children's education falls under their jurisdiction, namely the Bible part. But they can easily conceive of another part of their children's education, namely the "school" part, which lies outside of their jurisdiction. There exists a dividing wall, separating these two fields of knowledge and that particular division sits at the heart of many of our problems. One goal of this chapter is to don my best Ronald Reagan voice and proclaim, "Mr. Gorbachev, tear down this wall!"

In Ephesians 6:4, the Apostle Paul says, "And, ye fathers, provoke not your children to wrath: but bring them up in the nurture and admonition of the Lord." We see the same instruction at various places in the book of Proverbs, not the least of which is, "Train up a child in the way he should go: and when he is old, he will not depart from it" (Prov. 22:6). As further support for education being a ministry of the family, we see that discipline is a duty given to parents (Prov. 23:13; 13:24; Heb. 12:9-10). Those who reduce discipline to punishment may not see the significance of this point. The use of the rod is indeed corrective, but it is not punitive. The rod is not for punishment, but it is for training and education. The sword, by contrast, is a tool for punishment wielded by the state. The state does not educate with the sword. Parents do educate with the rod. And the Bible places that wonder wand of education in the hand of dad and mom. It follows that the family sphere, not the state or the church, maintain the ministry of education.

With this much established, we still need to know how to educate, and God's covenant of grace and the covenant household has much to say about how to educate.

Better yet, we should say that *the covenant has everything to do* with how we should educate. Consider the following lines from Geerhardus Vos. Speaking of the Reformed believer, he asks,

> How else could he receive and reflect the glory of his God, if he were not able to stand in the circle of light, where the beams penetrate to him from all sides? To stand in that circle means to be a party in the covenant, to live out of a consciousness of the covenant and to drink out of the fulness of the covenant. The Christian knows that he is a party in God's covenant and as such he has all things and spans at any one moment the whole orbit of grace, both in time and for eternity.[1]

Already we can see how this chapter on covenant education builds upon the previous ones, and without a grasp on both the covenant household and the covenant of grace as considered in previous chapters, the point of this chapter will be elusive. Vos maintains that the covenant member stands within the covenant as a "circle of light." Light helps you see. Standing in the light, you can understand. The covenant member not only stands in this circle: he lives out of a consciousness of this covenant in which he finds himself. His covenant membership is expansive, for as a party in God's covenant he "has all things." Moreover, his covenant membership not only informs eternity, but orients him to life "in time" and the things of the earth.

1. Vos, *Redemptive History and Biblical Interpretation*, 256–57.

Faith is the essential ingredient not only to the justification of a sinner but also to education, wisdom, and a life well lived amid the glory of God—"Whereas the Lutheran tends to view faith one-sidedly—only in its connection with justification—for the Reformed Christian it is saving faith in all the magnitude of the word."[2] In the covenantal outlook, faith embraces more than justification—"[Faith] lays hold of Christ as Prophet, Priest, and King, as his rich and full Messiah. The deepest reason for this difference in view is none other than the fact that the reception of the full glory of the work of God's grace in the consciousness of faith is the most important thing to the Reformed believer."[3]

The covenant household then is in God's covenant, the circle of light. The covenant children of such a house are both in the covenant house with their parents and siblings and in the covenant of grace. They are not outside, but grafted into the olive tree (Rom. 11) and Christ (John 15). Faith is essential, of course. Without faith, there is no justification. Without faith, there will be no "reception of the full glory of the work of God's grace."

A covenant education then involves covenant nurture. Covenant education teaches from within the covenant and faith is always an essential ingredient no matter the subject. You may be able to grasp that triangles have three sides without faith. But there is a purpose to triangles having three sides, and man can never grasp that telos

2. Ibid.
3. Ibid.

apart from faith. Educated men know what things are for. You might say that the educated know the beginning and the end, and the only way to know the Alpha and Omega is by faith (Rev. 22:13).

Contrast this vision of education with the approach of modern man. Modern man's approach appears in C.S. Lewis's book *The Discarded Image*. His point regarding cosmology can be laid over modern man's entire outlook. Lewis writes, "Hence to look out on the night sky with modern eyes is like looking out over a sea that fades away into mist."[4] The medievals did not think that way. Referring to Dante, Lewis writes, "He is like a man being conducted through an immense cathedral, not like one lost in a shoreless sea."[5]

To be conducted through an immense cathedral is to be *in something*, something like a circle of light. Lewis speaks on a cosmic level, referring to a cosmic cathedral, and this is a very different concept than being lost, alone on a boundless sea. The covenant child is born into a covenant home. There are clear borders to this home. He is born into God's covenant of grace (the ice cream shop from chapter 3), and this covenant also has clear borders. Lewis takes this border concept to a cosmic level, and note that the borders of these various "homes" are not prison walls. They are not rooms of ignorance with the truth existing outside. They are God-designed realms of blessing, light, and truth. I am not equating the borders

4. C.S. Lewis, *The Discarded Image* (New York: Harper Collins, 2013), 52.
5. Ibid., 53.

of the covenant of grace with the cosmic cathedral Lewis described. I am, however, marking a correlation in worldview. The cosmos, according to the medievals, was something that man is in. The covenant, according to the Reformed, is something that Christians are in. The modern conception of education involves one man exploring an endless and infinite world. He is free to choose his path, his major and minor with which he will equip himself to go his own way. But this whole picture is wrong. The world is neither infinite nor endless. When man explores by himself, he gets lost and eaten by bears nearly every time. This modern approach to education is doomed, for it is shot through with individualism and the deification of the cosmos. God says something very different, "My son, hear the instruction of thy father, and forsake not the law of thy mother" (Prov. 1:8). We are told to seek the wisdom from above (James 3:17). When we get educated in this wisdom, it does not terminate in ourselves but shows itself in our good works toward others (James 3:13). The covenant informs these passages of Scripture. A son is to hear the instruction of his father (the covenant household), and man is to listen to the wisdom of *the Father* who delivers wisdom from above (the covenant of grace).

Let's reason by way of analogy from Herman Bavinck. Speaking of our salvation, he writes,

Atonement, forgiveness, justification, the mystical union, sanctification, glorification, and so on—they do not come into being after and as a result of faith but are objectively, actively present in Christ. They are the fruits solely of his suffering and dying, and they are appropriated on our part by faith. . . . In God's own time they will also become the subjective possession of believers.[6]

Bavinck says that the blessings of our salvation are objectively and actively present in Christ. It is not as if we bring these blessings into existence by our faith. Rather, we "appropriate" by faith these blessings that already existed in Christ.

Consider how this maps on to education. What is truth? Well, the Bible has an answer to that question. Jesus says, "I am the way, *the truth*, and the life" (John 14:6). Likewise, all the treasures of wisdom and knowledge are found in Christ (Col. 2:3). You might ask, "Really, *all of them?*" The answer is, indeed, you won't find a scintilla of wisdom or knowledge outside of him. This truth sheds light on another, namely that the fear of the LORD is the beginning of wisdom (Prov. 9:10). You cannot obtain an ounce of wisdom without the fear of the Lord, and you cannot obtain an ounce of wisdom outside of Christ in whom all of the treasures of wisdom and knowledge are found. Hopefully, that dividing wall of hostility referenced before is starting to come down at this point. The oranges being examined in science class are Christ's oranges. The history is Christ's history, and so on.

6. Herman Bavinck, *Reformed Dogmatics*, 3:523.

The trouble is that most evangelicals attempt to educate children without reference to their covenant status, if not conceiving of them as outside of the covenant altogether. So the Christian teacher stands in the circle of light and he educates the child who stands outside of the circle of light. He raises the children to know *about* the Lord. But this is different than raising the child *in* the nurture and admonition of the Lord (Eph. 6:4).

There is an interesting comparison to C.S. Lewis's "Meditation in a Toolshed" at this point. Lewis speaks of standing in a dark toolshed and observing a sunbeam that came through the crack at the top of the door. He meditates on the difference between looking at the beam and along the beam. While looking at the beam, he says, "I was seeing the beam, not seeing things by it."[7] When he moved so that the beam fell on his eyes,

> Instantly the whole previous picture vanished. I saw no toolshed, and (above all) no beam. Instead I saw, framed in the irregular cranny at the top of the door, green leaves moving on the branches of a tree outside and beyond that, 90 odd million miles away, the sun. Looking along the beam, and looking at the beam are very different experiences.[8]

Covenant education raises children to look along the beam. And by that beam of light, they see. By that beam

7. C.S. Lewis, *God in the Dock* (New York: Harper Collins, 2014), kindle loc. 212.
8. Ibid.

of light, they understand the world around them, God, and themselves. The children do not observe the church as an outsider, studying its worship and sacraments at a distance. Granted, there is nothing wrong with looking at the beam. Lewis points out the benefits of such knowledge. The point is that such knowledge alone is insufficient. Covenant nurture raises children in the faith, in the worshiping community, in the covenant home, in the covenant of grace, and even in the cosmic cathedral that God their Father has made.

There's more to this covenantal education. We can't leave off the expansive nature of it. Let's take Vos's reference to a circle of light and make it our own. Vos speaks of a man inside a circle of light with the light penetrating him from all sides. But recall that he says this man has "all things." So you might say that the light of this circle shines forth to illuminate everything. It is by the light of this circle, the light of Christ and his covenant, that you not only have a consciousness of your salvation, but you can also understand the whole world God has made. This covenant roots us in history. It informs the very nature of family. It illuminates nature. It relates heaven and earth, the present and the future, the one and the many, the Creator and the creation.

This point regarding illumination by way of covenant applies to both morality and academics. On the moral front, there often remains in the mind of many Christians the sense that the church-raised children are ignorant. They have not experienced the world, the hard knocks and what not. This sentiment resides in various adults and in the children or youths themselves. I don't deny that there is a kernel of truth in this thinking. Children by definition have not reached maturity and the goal is for covenant children to go through life experientially ignorant of grievous sin. But we need to rework this construction outlined above. The covenant is not the place of ignorance, but the place of light, truth, and understanding. The darkness is outside.

A covenant education sheds light such that covenant children are rightly aware of the world's evils. They are not ignorant to the schemes of the devil, the strategy of the strange woman, or the transgressor's hard ways. It is those who are outside of covenant with God who are ignorant. They stumble over themselves knowing not what they are doing.

This truth applies to academic knowledge as well. Those in covenant with God are the ones positioned to understand their Father's handiwork. That old hymn was right:

This is my Father's world,
And to my listening ears
All nature sings, and round me rings
The music of the spheres.
This is my Father's world:
I rest me in the thought
Of rocks and trees, of skies and seas
His hand the wonders wrought.[9]

9. Maltbie D. Babcock, "This Is My Father's World," 1901.

Covenant education involves training children to know whose they are and where they are. It teaches children the word of the Father, be that special revelation or general revelation, and that word of the Father is grace to them because, as the old hymn says, the Father is *their Father*. In this sense, covenant children are raised not only to understand the works of the Creator, but the works of their very own Father. They receive knowledge of the blessings of God given to them in creation. So they are not outside observers at this point either. The things they learn about are gifts to them from their Father, for as Paul said, "For all things are yours; whether Paul, or Apollos, or Cephas, or the world, or life, or death, or things present, or things to come; all are yours; and ye are Christ's; and Christ *is* God's" (1 Cor. 3:21-23).

Grasp the covenantal tenor of the text: This is the covenantal tenor that ought to permeate covenantal education. We are not to take a text like this and tell a young son, "The world is yours buddy, all yours, go make what you will of it." You get this kind of aroma from Hollywood as they craft a scene of the teenage son setting off to college. They have part of the truth. The truth is that the world belongs to a people of which covenant children are a part, namely the covenant people. When Paul says, "For all things are *yours*," he is speaking in the plural. He is not referring to an individual, and he is not merely referring to the Corinthians. The context makes clear that he is speaking of the covenant people of God, the saints. All things belong to the covenant people. And they are Christ's and Christ is God's.

7 Covenant Dominion
We Shall Not Labor in Vain

One point that has been just behind the scenes through this book is the fact that covenant is related to cosmos, that is, an entire system of thought and, more to the point, an entire system for life. Covenant gets into just about everything. It is not merely an organizing theme for how the Scriptures come to us, which is massive enough. It is an organizing theme for life on earth. It orients you in the world. In other words, the covenant household has a purpose. That purpose goes all the way back to the beginning and fills up life like music does Carnegie Hall.

The central theme of this book has been that the solution for the dissolving American family is a restoration of the covenant household. But what happens when we do recover the covenant household? Just how big is this restoration project? The answer is, *cosmic.* While this book is truly about the family, it ends up being about far more. When God fulfills his promise to Abraham that "all the families of the earth shall be blessed," then you end up with a reformed earth, a baptized world, nations that have been taught to observe all of Christ's commands. You end up with covenant dominion.

The principles expounded throughout this work will not only reorient your approach to the family. Covenant grounds us in history and tradition. It provides us with a meaningful telos. It maintains the harmonious relationship between heaven and earth, the physical and the spiritual, the natural and the supernatural, the past and the future, justification and sanctification, the church and the world. It also recasts our present political divide as what it truly is, a manifestation of the enmity that exists between the seed of the woman and the seed of the serpent.

In this final chapter, I will demonstrate how Christians exercise covenantal dominion. My hope is that you will see with fresh encouragement that God remakes the world via covenant. To that end, we will take a look at the false religion arising in our midst that attempts to unmake the world. Then we will go back to the beginning when God first established the covenant of grace with our father Adam after his fall. From that fall, down through the corridors of history, God has been after the salvation of the world through covenant. Finally, we will consider faith as the key instrument for conquest in our long war against the serpent and his seed.

WHAT WE'RE UP AGAINST

I was recently put on to an article by the French political theorist Chantal Delsol entitled, "The End of Christianity."[1] I'd want to edit several things in Delsol's article, but her piece can help American Christians see the inevitability of religion informing society. It also highlights the false religion flowering all around us. Delsol writes, "At the start of the twenty-first century, the most established and most promising philosophical current is a form of cosmotheism."[2] Cosmotheism is the attribution of deity to the cosmos itself, contrary to Christianity which teaches that God is set apart from the cosmos.

Delsol continues—

Our Western contemporaries no longer believe in a beyond or in a transcendence. The meaning of life must therefore be found in this life itself, and not above it, where there is nothing. The sacred is found here: in the landscapes, in the life of the earth, and in humans themselves . . . Under cosmotheism, man feels at home in the world, which represents the only reality . . . Under monotheism, man feels a stranger in this immanent world and longs for the other world. For the monotheist, this world is only a temporary lodging. For the cosmotheist, it is a home. The postmodern mind is tired of living in a temporary lodging! It needs a home of its own . . . One becomes

1. Chantal Delsol, "The End of Christianity," Hungarian Conservative, October 29, 2021, https://www.hungarianconservative.com/articles/culture _society/the-end-of-christianity/.
2. Ibid.

a cosmotheist again because one wants to reintegrate oneself into this world as a full citizen.[3]

Delsol says that this world is only a temporary lodging for the monotheist, "I'm just traveling through." That sentiment is no doubt true, "We are strangers and pilgrims" who seek a "better country that is a heavenly one" (Heb. 11:13, 16). But we are not *merely* strangers and pilgrims on earth. Evangelicals know well that they are strangers and pilgrims. But they have not thought through what else they are. They are many other things, including members of the new humanity that has been formed in Christ. But evangelicals, by and large, view the world as nothing but temporary lodging. Additionally, the cosmotheist (that is, the pagan) is currently running in the other direction. The pagan is tired of temporary lodging. He wants a home in the world.

Let me come at the same idea from another direction. The vast majority of American Christians view life on earth like an individual sitting at a train station. He has his ticket to ride to heaven. He knows that he must be moral at this train station. He must read his Bible and say his prayers to the God who awaits him at his final destination. But this man has no sense that the glory of the heaven to which he is going is descending upon the train station. And it is. Jesus, after all, taught us to pray, "Your kingdom come your will be done on earth as it is in heaven."

3. Ibid.

Now, this man, having no idea that the glory of the heaven to which he is going is descending upon the train station, has no strategy for the train station. He doesn't know how to take dominion at the train station, and he doesn't know how his work and family at the train station connects with the God who has given him his ticket to ride the heavenly express. When this train-station-sitting man sees idols being set up all around him, he very often doesn't even get out of his seat, "This is the devil's playground after all . . . I'm just passing through."

Evangelicals think and live this way in part because God's covenant and the covenant household are not shaping our thought and life. Faithfulness is strengthened as we grasp what God is actually doing in the world, which means we must know him as the covenant-keeping God and ourselves as his covenant people. More particularly, we must know him as our covenant-keeping God from the time of our first father Adam.

COVENANT FROM THE BEGINNING

Many Christians think of God's covenantal dealings with man throughout history simply as a means through which he saves his elect. He certainly does no less. But he accomplishes more in his covenant with man. Remember our definition of the covenant of grace involves God constituting an organized people. These people worship him and serve as a kingdom of priests in the world (Exod. 19:6). Saints keep getting added to this organized people such that they cover the earth. It is not that you have scattered seeds of the woman who simply war against a spiritual seed of the serpent. Rather the seed of the woman are God's covenant people. We are bound together throughout the ages, warring against the seed of the serpent. God has signed and sealed his covenant people from the outset, indicating that the war between the two seeds is a public, covenantal affair.

In the very beginning, God made a covenant of life with our father Adam and his seed. This covenant of life was distinct from God's covenant of grace. God promised life and blessing to Adam and his posterity on condition of perfect and personal obedience. In this covenant of life, God told man to be fruitful and multiply, to fill the earth and have dominion. This dominion mandate was not a command placed upon solitary man. The work of dominion would necessarily require a family. It was within this very mandate that we hear it is not good for man to be alone (Gen. 2:18). Adam needed a helper suitable to him, for the work which God gave him called for such a helper. Indeed, he was to be fruitful, and he could not be without a wife and children, without a household.

The great tragedy is that mankind fell in our father Adam. This dominion would now not only be painful (pain in childbearing, thorns and thistles). Indeed it would be impossible for man left to himself.

Thus the covenant-word comes from God to Adam that the seed of the woman would bruise the head of the serpent (Gen. 3:15). How one takes this promise in Genesis 3:15 will have significant downstream consequences for how he approaches life in the world. One man sees Genesis 3:15 as simply a first annunciation of the gospel, not an establishment of the covenant of grace. Good news is proclaimed and individuals can believe this promise or not (i.e. ice cream stand in the street). Another take is to say that God is actually cutting the covenant of grace with Adam, constituting an organized people over and to whom he says, "I am your God and you are my people" (i.e. ice cream served via an ice cream shop).

The arguments that God not only announced the gospel, but actually announced it via an established post-fall covenant of grace with Adam can be categorized under the following heads: promise, sacrifice, sign, people, and condition.

First, God made a promise of grace in and by Jesus Christ when he said the seed of the woman would crush the head of the serpent. And this particular promise always comes in and through covenant. The Westminster Confession of Faith is helpful here as it explains that God's good news is announced *in the covenant of grace*—

> Man by his fall having made himself incapable of life by that covenant, the Lord was pleased to make a second, commonly called the covenant of grace: wherein he freely offered unto sinners life and salvation by Jesus Christ, requiring of them faith in him that they may be saved, and promising to give unto all those that are ordained unto life his Holy Spirit, to make them willing and able to believe.[4]

4. Philip Schaff, *The Creeds of Christendom* (Grand Rapids: Baker Book House, 1985), 617.

So, yes, God offered sinful Adam and Eve salvation by Jesus Christ in Genesis 3:15. But *wherein* did he offer them that salvation? He offered them that salvation in the covenant of grace that he established with them.

Second, Adam's posterity is immediately found offering sacrifices. They were not merely relating to God, but worshipping and communing with God through sacrificial worship according to God's covenantal design.

Moreover, while baptism had not yet come, and neither had circumcision, even this first establishment of God's covenant promise was not without a sign. The covenant theologian Herman Witsius has said,

> It appears more than probable to us, with some very learned men, from the Mosaic history, that immediately upon the promulgation of the covenant of grace, Adam, at the command of God, slew beasts for sacrifice, who skins were, by the favor of God, granted to him and his wife for clothing: which was not without its mystical signification.[5]

Strikingly, God's covenant of grace with Adam established immediately upon the fall maintained the principle of blessing upon his seed, for there would be enmity between the seed of the woman and the seed of the serpent. From the very beginning, then, God was concerned with the household and a public covenant people on earth. Indeed, John Owen has said, "The first church among

5. Herman Witsius, *Economy of the Covenants*, vol. 1 (Grand Rapids: Reformation Heritage), 309.

fallen sinners was established in the family of Adam; and, in accord with that theological norm which I have set out, its prime purpose was the organization of a visible assembly of people, worshipping God in the person of the Mediator."[6] He adds, "At this time [Adam's] family constituted the Church of God and, at the same time, the entire human race."[7] Cain himself was a covenant member and member of the church visible before being exiled from it—"With the infidelity and hypocrisy of Cain so openly exposed, he could no longer be tolerated within the bosom of the Church."[8]

The fifth support for God cutting the covenant of grace with Adam involves the presence of conditions. We see that an obedient faith, which is the condition of the covenant of grace, was operating as a covenantal condition even at this early date. God told Cain, even after he murdered his brother, "If thou doest well, shalt thou not be accepted? and if thou doest not well, sin lieth at the door" (Gen. 4:7). John Ball explains that this word from God to Cain came by virtue of the covenant of grace,

> By virtue of this Covenant, Cain as well as Abel offered sacrifice unto God, as a member of the church, and after his sacrifice was rejected he hears from God, *If thou do well shalt thou not be accepted?* which is a promise of the

6. John Owen, *Biblical Theology* (Morgan, PA: Soli Deo Gloria Publications, 1996), 184.
7. Ibid., 184.
8. Ibid., 188.

covenant that took place after the fall; for the former covenant [the covenant of life] made no mention of mercy to
be vouchsafed to the delinquent upon repentance, nor of
acceptance after transgression.[9]

Likewise, we see the condition of this obedient faith
in Abel's sacrifice. Hebrews 11:4 tells us, "By faith Abel
offered unto God a more excellent sacrifice than Cain, by
which he obtained witness that he was righteous."

Now, why so many supports for the covenant of grace
being cut with Adam? Good question. I'm glad you asked.
And I must reply to your question with my own. What
kind of world are you living in? Do you live in a world
where God merely saves individuals through individual
promises to them? Or do you live in a world where God
has always announced good news via cut covenant? Has
God simply been saving people out of a fallen world, for-
giving them of their sins through faith in his son? Or has
he, in addition to all of that, been constituting a new humanity, a worshipping and redeemed community of families, a signed and sealed people on earth who historically
and victoriously war against the seed of the serpent?

I'm commending this latter and fulsome vision as an
accurate picture of reality. All of that is baked into the
simple and familiar phrase—"For God sent not his Son
into the world to condemn the world; but that the world
through him might be saved" (John 3:17).

9. Ball, *A Treatise of the Covenant of Grace*, 43.

THE COVENANT HOUSEHOLD AND THE WAR FOR THE COSMOS

It is no surprise then that when God reestablishes this covenant of grace with Noah, Abraham, Moses, David, and Christ in the New Covenant, the covenant household and the war for the cosmos is always in view.[10]

When God cuts covenant with Noah, he reiterates the dominion mandate and makes covenant not only with Noah but his sons also (Gen. 9:8-9).

As we have seen in Abraham, not only will people be blessed, but the "families of the earth will be blessed" (Gen. 12:3). The covenant people were publicized for like the sacrifice that God commanded Adam in the beginning which resulted in him and his wife, and indeed their children after them, being clothed, and like the rainbow which was the Noahic sign seen not merely by Noah but his household, so the covenant sign of circumcision was divinely administered to Abraham and his seed. Furthermore, dominion is present in the Abrahamic covenant for God promised him a great nation and kings from his loins (Gen. 12:2; 17:6).

The Mosaic administration continues this same theme. Parents were to teach God's law to their children diligently (Deut. 6:7). Passover was observed for an ordinance to the Israelites and their sons (Exod. 12:24). Along these lines, respected reformed theologians, Louis Berkhof being an example, have pointed out that children indeed ate

10. See C.R. Wiley, *The Household and the War for the Cosmos* (Moscow, ID: Canon Press, 2019).

the Passover. It follows that the children partook of the paschal lamb which was a means by which the covenant of grace was administered (WCF 7.5).

Similarly, the covenant theologian, John Ball, said of the Mosaic covenant, "This Covenant God made not only with the Fathers, whom he brought out of the Land of Egypt, but with their posterity."[11] He proceeds to cite Deuteronomy 29:10-12,

> Ye stand this day all of you before the Lord your God; your captains of your tribes, your elders, and your officers, *with* all the men of Israel, *Your little ones, your wives,* and thy stranger that *is* in thy camp, from the hewer of thy wood unto the drawer of thy water: *That thou shouldest enter into covenant with the Lord thy God,* and into his oath, which the Lord thy God maketh with thee this day. [emphasis mine]

These words from Moses not only prove the covenant household's organic tie with the covenant of grace. They also establish conquest in and through this covenant of grace. Israel stood on the banks of the Jordan River, soon to cross over and conquer giants in the land. Every administration of the covenant of grace not only preserves the principle and coming seed, the Lord Jesus Christ who would ultimately crush the head of the snake. They also fulfill the promise that the seed of the woman, the children of God, would war against the serpent's seed.

11. Ball, *A Treatise of the Covenant of Grace*, 129.

Indeed, God would crush Satan under the covenant people's feet as well (Rom. 16:20).

The conquering covenant household appears in the Davidic administration of the covenant of grace as well. For the promise there was that "thine house and thy kingdom shall be established for ever before thee" (2 Sam. 7:16), and "I will set up they seed after thee, which shall proceed out of thy bowels, and I will establish his kingdom" (2 Sam. 7:12). Again, the chief seed is Christ. So it is with Adam's seed in Genesis 3:15. So it is with Abraham's seed (Gal. 3:16). And so it is with the Mosaic administration (Luke 22:15). But our Lord Jesus Christ is not the only seed in view throughout these various covenants. In each, the children which do not degenerate into the seed of the serpent are at enmity with the seed of the serpent, having God as their God, eating the lamb, sitting on thrones, and all of this by faith.

This language of those who "do not degenerate into the seed of the Serpent" comes from the respected theologian John Ball. For example, he writes,

In the former Covenant [by which Ball means the covenant of grace made with Adam] a secret honor was put upon Eve, as she was made (if we may so speak) the first pipe whereby God conveyed the grace of his Covenant unto her posterity, who did not degenerate into the seed of the Serpent.[12]

12. Ball, *A Treatise of the Covenant of Grace*, 50.

The language of "degenerate" should not be taken to mean the loss of the Spirit's work of regeneration unto new life, which, of course, once worked in a man cannot be lost.

Moreover, Ball's point is not that salvation runs down bloodlines. I will quote him at length on this point so that the organic nature of the covenant might be grasped while maintaining the necessity of faith (which itself will be addressed more in a moment). Picking up on the heels of his "Eve as a pipe" comment and shifting to the Abrahamic covenant, Ball writes—

> But here the Covenant is made with Abraham, who received it, not as an example only, nor as a type, but as an Ordinance leading unto the conveyance of the same Covenant to all the confederates. In which sense it is plainly spoken to in the Epistles to the Romans and Galatians. [A]nd he [is] called the Father of the faithful (Romans 4:11, 12, 16). And they which are of the faith the children of Abraham (Galatians 3:7), the seed of Abraham (Galatians 3:29). Abraham is not the Father of the faithful effectively, as if he should be the worker of faith in all, or that men should be borne faithful of him: For so God only by the holy Ghost is the Father of the faithful: But analogically for the grace of the Covenant given unto him on that condition and privilege, that as Fathers transfer and pass over their rights and inheritance to their children: so he as a Father should propagate the righteousness of faith and free blessedness to all

the faithful by Doctrine, Example and Covenant. So that all who receive this Covenant from God in Christ, doe likewise by faith draw it through Abraham, to whom the promise was made, Galatians 3:16.[13]

THE SECOND ADAM

We must, then, never presume that any blessing will come to our household, our seed, apart from Christ. As Ball notes above, the only way to receive this covenant from God is "in Christ." He is the principle seed and in him all things hold together. It follows that outside of him everything falls apart, including our homes. Jesus is not only the son of God. He is also the son of man. Indeed he is the second Adam, and where the first Adam was merely a living soul, the second is a life-giving spirit (1 Cor. 15:45).

This life-giving spirit did not consider equality with God a thing to be grasped. He was born of the Virgin Mary, suffered under Pontius Pilate, was crucified, died and was buried. He descended into Hades. He conquered sin, death, and the grave. He has risen never to die again. His blood is the blood of the New Covenant. And the terms of that New Covenant are blood-anchored: Believe in the Lord Jesus Christ and you will be saved.

There is no way to fulfill the original dominion mandate apart from this Christ, and there is no way to live faithfully under the blessing of God apart from him.

13. Ibid.

Indeed, through our father Adam, our first representative, we inherited both moral corruption and guilt. In this condition, neither we or anyone in our household can be reconciled to God on our own merits or in our own strength. We need something to come to us from outside of us. We need what only God can supply. We need his very righteousness, not our own, and every member in our covenant household needs the righteousness of God through faith in Christ for "there is no other name under heaven given among men by which we must be saved" (Acts 4:12).

FAITH

It is fitting that we conclude this book on the covenant household with an emphasis on faith. Faith is how the covenant has always been kept. On the one hand you have parents who presume upon God, by which I mean that they do not actually trust God to bless their children while raising them in the nurture and admonition of the Lord. Rather these presuming parents simply assume God will bless their children regardless of faith and obedience. On the other hand, there are the parents who simply do not believe that God has promised their children anything. They have bought into the hyper-individualism of our times and mistakenly assume that God only promised Abraham that he would bless his children, and this pattern of "blessing upon the seed" does not carry down to us, the children of Abraham.

Avoiding both of these pitfalls is the way forward. And that means we simply must trust God's promises to us and to our children. We must be like our father Abraham who believed God when he said that he would be God to him and to his seed after him in their generations. For that matter, we must be like our father Adam who named his wife "mother of all the living" after he heard God's covenant promise regarding his seed crushing the head of the serpent. Adam believed God that he would not ultimately die; the serpent would not win in the end. We must be like faithful Israel under the Mosaic covenant who conquered the land and taught their children and fed them the Passover meal with instruction as to its meaning. We must be like David who ruled in the fear of God and believed God that his seed would sit on thrones. We have warrant to trust that God will bless our households for as Peter said, "The promise is unto you and to your children" (Acts 2:39).

This very faith was active in Joshua. He was not a micromanaging, gripping, domineering man. He believed what God had already revealed and said, "As for me and my house we will serve the Lord." Faith is the key ingredient, and here is a check to those who would move forward without faith: the covenant has always been kept by faith and "without faith it is impossible to please God" (Heb. 11:6).

Beware, for there have regularly been those who draw near the Lord with their mouth and with their lips honor him, but have removed their hearts far from him (Isa.

29:13). We see this superficiality around us in nearly every direction. It is this very superficiality that has led to the dissolution of the covenant home and the vanity and barrenness of our present age. But, in the midst of these ruins in which we stand, with the trappings of a former Christian civilization strewn about here in the West, God himself has promised the saints:

> And they shall build houses, and inhabit them; And they shall plant vineyards, and eat the fruit of them. They shall not build, and another inhabit; They shall not plant, and another eat: For as the days of a tree are the days of my people, And mine elect shall long enjoy the work of their hands. They shall not labour in vain, Nor bring forth for trouble; For they are the seed of the blessed of the LORD, And their offspring with them. (Isa. 65:21-23)

Notice what God's covenant people do. They build. They plant. They work with their hands. Their faith is not that false faith which fails to work. They have a living faith, an obedient faith. By faith, they conquer. Their faith is in Christ and indeed they are saved through this faith. But their faith also apprehends all of God's covenant promises. We have seen that those covenant promises are vast. They include life and blessing for our children, and our children's children to a thousand generations. They include the conquest and salvation of the whole world. They include the sworn oath from God that our works of faith and labors of love will not come up empty.

How can we go forward with confidence that we will not labor in vain? How can we be sure that we will not bring forth for trouble? They, the elect, are the seed of the blessed of the LORD *and their offspring with them*—

Blessed is every one that feareth the LORD; that walketh in his ways. For thou shalt eat the labour of thine hands: happy shalt thou be, and it shall be well with thee. Thy wife shall be as a fruitful vine by the sides of thine house: thy children like olive plants round about thy table. (Ps. 128:1-3)

Conclusion

What Chesterton once said of his own book applies just the same to my own—"I will not call it my philosophy; for I did not make it. God and humanity made it; and it made me."[1] I have not presented anything new in these pages. I have not created anything. Instead, this book has been more like describing my mother. I discovered this mother covenant later in life but she has been there all along. That discovery is deeply humbling and delightful. Immense gratitude swells for parents, grandparents, and great grandparents who have kept covenant by faith and raised children in the nurture and admonition of the Lord. Immense gratitude swells for God our Father who is the covenant keeping God who shows mercy to thousands of them that love him and keep his commandments (Exod. 20:6).

1. Chesterton, *Orthodoxy*, 19.

My hope is that God grants you similar gratitude through your reading of this book. My hope is that your faith will be strengthened and you will be steadied in a time of upheaval, solidified in a time of dissolution and fragmentation. And my hope is that the truth expounded in this book undergirds and strengthens Christian families such that we see a glorious fulfillment of God's covenant promises leading to reformation and revival in our thirsty land.

Given the nature of the topic, there are certainly objections that many faithful saints may raise to various points that I have made throughout this work. I have not raised or addressed many of those objections. As I noted at the outset, I have simply intended to cut away some of the overgrowth that has covered up this Old Covenantal path. Or to change the metaphor, I have sought by God's help and word to shine some light on the path that our fathers and mothers have walked for centuries, a path that you too, like myself, may very well have already been walking even if unknowingly—

And these all, having obtained a good report through faith, received not the promise: God having provided some better thing for us, that they without us should not be made perfect. Wherefore seeing we also are compassed about with so great a cloud of witnesses, let us lay aside every weight, and the sin which doth so easily beset us, and let us run with patience the race that is set before us, looking unto Jesus the author and finisher of our faith. (Heb. 11:39-12:2)

Made in United States
Orlando, FL
05 June 2023

33807611R00082